The Unit Study
Idea Book

By Valerie Bendt

Other books by Valerie Bendt:

How To Create Your Own Unit Study
Creating Books With Children
The Frances Study Guide
Success With Unit Studies
For the Love of Reading

Cover photo courtesy of *The Image Bank*

P.O. Box 1365
8786 Highway 21
Melrose, FL 32666

ISBN 1-880892-42-1

DEDICATION

This book is dedicated to my loving husband, Bruce, and my five wonderful children, who are also my friends, students, and often my instructors!

The children's names and ages at the time of publication are as follows: Michelle, 12 years old; Melissa, 10 years old; Robert, 8 years old; Raymond, 6 years old; and Mandy, 2 years old.

TABLE OF CONTENTS

INTRODUCTION

This book is meant to be a book of ideas, not a curriculum guide. It is my hope that my ideas will serve as a catalyst to begin a chain reaction which will fuel your own ideas. Each one of us views things a little differently, and therefore we will be inspired to take a variety of avenues in our educational endeavors. This book is not meant to be exhaustive by any means, only inspiring and encouraging.

Many suggestions are given for each topic. Use only the suggestions that appeal to you. Your success will be greater if you enjoy what you are doing. Take one step at a time, not rushing through one project or task just to begin another. Realize that completing even **one** section or **one** project is a tremendous accomplishment. One single aspect of a unit is valuable and can stand on its own merits.

You will never be able to exhaust any given topic. Our Heavenly Father created such a vast and complex universe that even in a thousand lifetimes we could never learn all there is to know. Fortunately we are not limited by our lives here on earth, but have eternity to devote to our quest for knowledge of the Holy One and all that His works encompass.

It should be our desire to acquaint our children with a variety of ideas, people, and places. There is no set curriculum that should be imposed on all children. Children are individuals and therefore their studies should be tailored to meet their particular needs and desires. Our Lord has given parents charge over their children, and therefore we are our children's best curriculum designers. Our studies should not focus on our interest areas alone. Rather, areas of interest are broadened as we dare to investigate unexplored topics. However, our emphasis in these new study areas can be centered on those disciplines we favor most.

I have chosen to compile this book in a very simple manner. As I plan units throughout the year, I try to choose topics from a variety of subject areas. Although a number of content areas are integrated into each unit, the main thrust of a particular unit lies in a specific area. For example, I choose units primarily based on history, geography, science, math, fine arts, or literature. Each unit is written in a manner to encompass one content area. I feel that selecting from a variety of key study areas enables us to achieve a well rounded course of study.

It is my observation that many unit study curriculums overextend themselves as they try to integrate every discipline into each unit of study. This is often forced, and therefore the material integrated doesn't always make sense or truly benefit the study. It doesn't require the integration of all the content areas to be a valuable study. Some studies naturally lend themselves well to the integration of several content areas. I find that only a well-planned, un-inspiring, no-room-for-creative-input, type of unit study can satisfactorily integrate every subject. So stop worrying about your children getting their daily shot in the arm of math, science, history, language, art, music, geography, and spelling. Let's get on with real learning and real life that isn't compartmentalized into digestible doses of mediocrity. Still worried that your children will be lacking if they miss out on all these content areas? We must realize that the educational leaders in our society are trying to press our children into a mold to acquire the same (boring) skills. These skills have been allowed to overshadow true knowledge. Break the mold and allow a masterpiece to emerge!

Remember that this is only a book of ideas. Use your heart and mind to discern the path your family should take. Education does not need to be a complicated process, only a thoughtful one. May the Lord bless you in your desire to raise children for His glory.

SUGGESTIONS FOR MAKING THIS BOOK
EASIER TO USE

I encourage you to read my first book, *How to Create Your Own Unit Study*, before attempting to use this book. It will provide you with pertinent information which will help you to receive the full benefit from this unit study idea book.

Although suggested library books are given for each unit, they are not meant to be a stumbling block in the event that you cannot locate some of them. In my book *How to Create Your Own Unit Study*, a section is included on **"Using the Library"** along with a **"Library Reference Guide."** The information given will enable you to find books from your own library that pertain to each unit. Don't waste valuable time trying to locate books not owned by your library system. Use books available to you.

You may want to buy some books or materials to supplement your unit studies. Although it would be ideal to rely totally on your public library as a source for materials, this cannot always be done. However, if you are not buying textbooks and workbooks each year, it is easier to accommodate these occasional purchases.

I strongly urge you to buy *Books Children Love*, by Elizabeth Wilson. This is a fabulous resource for locating interesting and morally sound books relating to your topic of study. I have had good success in finding the books in my public library that are suggested in *Books Children Love*.

In this book of ideas, I list several activities and projects. This listing is meant to be a sampling from which you may choose. Don't try to undertake every suggestion. Too many activities and projects can be frustrating. Pace yourself, and most of all relax and enjoy your family!

LITERATURE

LIBRARY UNIT

This is a good unit to help you and your children get acquainted with the library. You may also want to arrange a guided tour of your public library. Try to visit the largest library in your area, as they will have the most services available.

Some churches maintain a library which is open to the general public for a small annual fee. Many homeschool support groups offer memberships for their lending libraries. As more people join, more materials can be purchased.

Resources

The Teaching Home magazine, April/May 1990, has an excellent section entitled **"Using the Library."** It includes topics from **Alternative Libraries** to **How to Teach Your Child to Do Research**. (See resource section for ordering information.)

Library Books

Libraries and You, by Pekay Shor. *Libraries and How to Use Them*, by Jeanne Hardendorff. *Check It Out! The Book About Libraries*, by Gail Gibbons. *The Way Things Work*, by David Macaulay, contains information about the printing press and book binding.

History

In 2700 B.C., the **Sumerians** established libraries to house tablets. One of the most famous of these libraries was built by the Babylonians in Nineveh. **Ptolemy I** established a library at Alexandria about 300 B.C. during the Greek rule in Egypt. **Eumenes II** (ruling from 197-159 B.C.) established a library at Pergamum, in northwest Asia Minor. By the 2nd century A.D., there were more than 25 public libraries in Rome. During invasions of the Roman Empire in the 3rd century, many libraries were burned. Monasteries served as safeguards for culture and education. Read about **St. Benedict** during the Dark Ages. During the 11th, 12th, and 13th centuries, many universities were founded and libraries were needed. It was difficult to obtain books because hand-copying was slow. Many books were chained to the shelves as they were extremely valuable. Later, **Johann Gutenburg** (1398?-1468), a German inventor developed moveable type and later the printing press . This made it possible to print large quantities of books at affordable prices. He printed the Gutenberg Bible in 1456. The Vatican Library was founded in the 15th century by **Pope Nicholas V. Reverend John Harvard** began the library at Harvard College. In 1731, **Benjamin Franklin** began a subscription library. **The Library of Congress** in Washington, D.C., was founded in 1800. The first free public libraries did not come about until the 19th century and were supported by taxes. As early as 1910, the first motorized book-mobiles were delivering reading material to people in rural communities. Read about **Melvil Dewey**, a librarian who worked out a number system used in many libraries today. It is called the Dewey Decimal Classification System. There is another classification scheme used called the Library of Congress Classification. You may wish to zero in on a couple of individuals during this study, such as Gutenberg and Dewey by reading biographies about these individuals. The rest can be summarized by reading about the history of libraries in an encyclopedia.

Terminology

Use the glossary in a library book such as **Libraries and You**, by Shor, or use a dictionary to define the following terms before you advance in the unit study. Children may write the term on one side of an index card and the definition on the other side. These terms are: author card, bibliography, biography, call number, card catalog, Dewey Decimal number, fiction, index, Library of Congress, nonfiction, periodical, subject card, table of contents, and title card.

Activities

Visit your local library and have your children make a map of the interior. Have them include sections for fiction, nonfiction, easy readers, biographies, fine arts, fairy tales, records, audio cassettes, video cassettes, paintings, periodical indexes, computers, and so on. Also remind them to put in restrooms, tables, chairs, display cases, etc. If your children are young or your library is large, you may want to only have your children map out the youth department. This pictorial representation should help to familiarize them with the layout of the library.

Library Skills

Teach your children to read numbers containing several decimal places. Give them a list of such numbers to put in numerical order. Check out a number of books from each section of the youth department of your public library. (Older students may choose books from other areas in the library as well.) Assign books to each child and have them make catalog cards for their books using 3x5 index cards. Show your children examples of the catalog cards found in one of the suggested library books. Explain about author, title, and subject cards. Have them make a subject, title, and author card for each book. Some books may have more than one subject card. Help your children to determine the subject matter for each book. You will note that each type of card contains a brief description of the book. If your children have not read the books, they can read the inside front jacket flap for information about the book.

Libraries vary in the arrangement of their card catalogs. Commonly they have a separate catalog for the subject cards, and the author and title cards are located in one catalog. Let each child take a turn at alphabetizing the cards they have made. You may want to combine all the cards, or separate them into groups by author, title, and subject before alphabetizing.

Once you've done this, your children may want to play "library." They can take turns "checking out" books. Place a slip of paper in the back of each book to be stamped when it is checked out. The children can also make their own library cards. All the activities mentioned above can be done with books you own as well as with library books. Use the Dewey Decimal Classification System (found in one of your library books on using the library) to determine call numbers. Remember, fiction as well as easy readers are classified by the author's last name.

Have each child make a book jacket to accompany his favorite book. These can be placed in your "library display case." The children can choose a book to read aloud and record on tape. A bell or musical instrument can be used to indicate that a page needs to be turned. This also provides hours of entertainment for toddlers who want to be read to frequently. They can listen to the tapes, and this will afford you extra time to help the older children with special schooling needs. A more complicated task would be to dramatize the story while making the tape. Children can be very creative when it comes to devising methods to simulate various sounds. Try it for fun sometime. You may find it helpful to check out a dramatized recording of a book from your library.

This is a good time to explain the parts of a book to your children. Begin with the cover or book jacket. Discuss the title, author, illustrator, and publisher. Point out that this information is on the spine of the book as well, and if it is a library book, point out the call number, too. Explain that the front inside jacket cover gives a brief description of the book. The back inside jacket cover tells

4

about the author and illustrator (if applicable.) Often the back outside cover will contain brief reviews of the book.

Examine the title page. If there are two title pages, compare them. Point out the copyright, Library of Congress number, publisher, and other information listed. Many books indicate whether the book is fiction, nonfiction, or a biography on the same page as the copyright. Discuss the dedication, introduction, preface, acknowledgements, etc. Talk about the table of contents, and have the children locate a desired chapter or section of the book. Discuss other significant parts of books such as the appendix, bibliography, and glossary. Locate books that contain these different sections.

Most books begin page one as a right-hand page. See if you can find any exceptions. Choose a book with an index. Explain that this is a listing of information that can be found in this particular book; it is in alphabetical order. Select several topics for your children to locate using the index. Find a book containing several different indexes. A poetry volume is a good choice. Choose one with a subject, author, and title index. Some poetry volumes have first line indexes, as well.

Have the children locate poems relating to specific topics such as cats, lightning, mountains, etc. Then have them use the other indexes in the volume.

Read several of the books that you have chosen to conduct this unit with your children. These may be factual books about the library, or they may be books you have chosen to "catalog." Allow each child to select a book to be presented to the family as an oral narration. They can pretend they are the librarian giving a book talk.

The children's reference section is an interesting place to explore in your public library. For information concerning this, read the **"Guide to the Reference Section of the Children's Department of the Public Library"** in my book *How to Create Your Own Unit Study*. This section will help you locate specific books pertaining to a particular unit study.

In my book, *How to Create Your Own Unit Study*, I included a sample of a children's authors unit we did a few years ago. Since that time, we have done several children's authors units in conjunction with my children writing and illustrating their own books. Studying various authors, their writing styles, their works, and their lives has given my children a wealth of information to draw from in creating their own books. We also studied select illustrators, including some author-illustrators. I have seen vast improvement in my children's writing and drawing. Vocabulary is more vivid, storylines are more involved and interesting, and more attention is given to details. Their drawings show more skill, effort, and imagination.

The books developed by the children are carefully made, using art quality paper, markers, paints, cardboard for stiffening covers, and button thread for handsewing the bindings. Six full weeks are taken to complete this project. The reward for this diligence is a collection of books that will be treasured for a lifetime. Yearbooks such as these provide a record of the children's progress and achievements. These books are something they can be proud of and will make a handsome addition to their portfolios.

I encourage you to assist your children in making these professional quality, handmade books. Over the years we have made a variety of books using a number of book-making manuals. Since these manuals are written for the traditional classroom, I find that some of them are difficult to adapt to my homeschool classroom. Some of these books present a secular philosophy of education that is contrary to my biblical philosophy of education.

After gaining several years of experience in making books with my children, I decided to write my own book-making manual entitled, *Creating Books with Children*. This book is written as a six-week book-making unit study, and it includes reproductions from more than 50 books made by homeschooled children. The book chapters include:

Week One:	Pre-Writing Activities
Week Two:	Writing the Stories
Week Three:	Text Layout and Editing
Week Four:	Illustrating the Books
Week Five:	Developing the Beginning and Ending Pages and the Book Jackets
Week Six:	Assembling the Books

(My books are available where Family Learning Center products are sold.)

There are other books designed to help you make less complicated books. A book that we have used and enjoyed is *How to Make Books With Children*, published by the Evan-Moor Corporation. This book is to be used primarily with young children. *Creating Books with Children* can be adapted to be used with all ages. For example, the younger children can dictate their stories to Mom or an older sibling. This is a helpful tip for any child who cannot write or who finds writing laborious. Even young children can assist in putting the books together and learn much about the mechanics of book assembly. Additional information about book binding can be found in David Macaulay's book, *The Way Things Work*. It also includes an explanation of the printing press. In *Creating Books with Children*, I stress that the final stories should be typed, resulting in a more professional-looking product. My capable children type their stories as well as assist me in typing the younger children's stories. This affords them extra typing practice, and it helps me out considerably. If you don't own a computer, wordprocessor or typewriter, consider investing in one. Typing skills are important and can be learned on a typewriter (preferably electric). Later these skills can be transferred over to use on a computer. If necessary, you can hire someone, maybe a fellow homeschooler, to type your children's stories.

This past year we chose to study two European children's authors. We studied Robert Louis Stevenson and Hans Christian Andersen. Robert Louis Stevenson was born in Scotland in 1850. We read his famous novel, *Treasure Island*, in an unabridged form. Although the language was somewhat complicated, the children enjoyed the book, especially my two boys. I read this book aloud to the children, and my two older girls occasionally read aloud also. We watched the movie *Treasure Island* and compared it with the book. We also checked out some library books on boats, as we encountered many navigational terms during our readings. We briefly studied pirates, using the *Pirates and Buccaneers Coloring Book* by Dover Publications, Inc. This interesting book includes pictures and historical information on pirates, buccaneers, and privateers.

We produced a video of an excerpt from *Treasure Island* entitled, "What I Heard in the Apple Barrel." This selection was found in the book *Play a Part*, by Bernice Carlson. Each child helped cut out and sew the costumes. My oldest daughter Michelle filmed the production and my daughter Melissa was the narrator. My two boys along with two other homeschooled boys made up the cast.

The boys copied some of their lines from the play as a writing and memory activity.

While studying Robert Louis Stevenson, we also read his book, *A Child's Garden of Verses*. Each child chose a number of poems to read aloud. Some of these poems were copied, and I dictated several poems to the children. I had the children make a list of words relating to childhood. Then they found rhyming words for each word in their list. Following this activity, they wrote poems about childhood and illustrated their poems. My girls then typed the poems and we glued them onto their illustrations.

I couldn't find a suitable biography about Stevenson, so we read the biographical information found in our encyclopedia. It was interesting to find that he became a proficient writer in his youth because he practiced "day in and day out." Wherever he went he carried two books, one to read and another to write in.

We also studied Hans Christian Andersen. We read a biography of his life that was very interesting entitled, *The Story of Hans Christian Andersen, Swan of Denmark*, by Ruth Manning-Sanders. We read many of his works which were located with the fairy tales in the library. We noticed there were several versions of each book; some were translated and illustrated by different individuals.

Andersen was born in Denmark, therefore his books were originally written in Danish. It is interesting to get two different translations of the same tale and compare them. Sometimes the titles are slightly different also. For example, *The Steadfast Tin Soldier* and *The Brave Tin Soldier*. Some translators choose to oversimplify the tales for younger children. After studying a few different versions of Andersen's Tales, I had the children retell the tale in their own words.

Some of the tales we read were: *The Nightingale, The Emperor's New Clothes, The Snow Queen, The Steadfast Tin Soldier, The Swineherd*, and *The Ugly Duckling*. I had the children read these aloud. Sometimes they made illustrations to accompany the tales. I also had each child write and illustrate their own fairy tale.

Andersen's tales provide excellent material for discussion. As you read the biography of Andersen and some of his well-known tales, you will begin to see why he wrote the tales. The tale, *The Ugly Duckling*, is said to be an autobiographical account of Andersen's life. As a child Andersen was unattractive and strange. He lived in a dream world of his own. He was teased and tormented by other children. Through his determination though, he became a famous writer and in later life dined with kings and queens.

Andersen often told his tales in the palaces of kings and queens; therefore, he used them frequently as subjects for his stories. One good example of this is the tale, **The Emperor's New Clothes**. Perhaps Andersen was trying to convey to the people in the king's court that they should learn to think for themselves. This story also provides a good opportunity to utilize some math skills. It was said that the Emperor had a different suit for each hour of the day. Have the children figure out how many suits he would wear in a day, week, month, and year. As you read his other tales, you will find interesting ideas to discuss with your children.

After studying these two authors, my children began writing their stories for their book projects. Since we had studied quite a bit about Stevenson, I thought they might like to write about pirates. My two older girls composed their stories on their own while my younger boys dictated their stories to me. This took about one week. My oldest daughter Michelle wrote a pirate story, but I could tell she wasn't really happy with it. I told her to write about anything she wanted. She chose to write a storybook for her baby sister Mandy entitled, **Mandy's Day at the Zoo**. Michelle has a strong interest in art; therefore she focused primarily on her illustrations. After she had written her story I read it and helped her edit it. I had her rewrite the story in present tense. She had written in past tense as if Mandy was telling the story. After she wrote it in present tense with Mandy still telling the story, Michelle said she realized that it sounded much better this way. Then Michelle typed her story on our word processor.

Melissa wrote a story about a little boy who was searching for buried treasure in his backyard. She was very descriptive in her account of his expeditions. She typed her story on the word processor, and I helped her with the punctuation which is her most difficult area. Melissa concentrated a lot on her illustrations, looking through some books to find pictures to aid her. She didn't trace the pictures, but she used them as examples for some of her drawings. Since she types and spells better than I do, she helped me type my boy's stories.

I was very encouraged to see the progress that Robert and Raymond had made in the year's time since they wrote and illustrated their first books. Their choice of vocabulary and their story content showed great advancements. I was also amazed at how they were able to carry an underlying theme throughout their stories. This is something we had discussed only briefly as we read other books. Each day I was more and more amazed as they dictated their stories to me. Even I was anxious to find out how their stories would end. It was also exciting to see the evidence of their personalities in their stories.

Raymond thought he was going to write a three hundred page novel. After writing eighteen pages on notebook paper that Raymond had dictated to me, I informed him that he'd better wrap up the story. He said he would end it, but that he was going to write a sequel! Very quickly he came up with a terrific ending that surprised me.

Robert's story was almost as long. Since my hand was worn out, he dictated much of his story to his sister Melissa. I was amazed at how Robert managed to keep three different parts of the story going at once. He used phrases such as, "Meanwhile back at the palace..." and "Out in the middle of the ocean...." He had so many ships and subplots that it was fascinating to see how he kept track of them all and managed to wind up the entire story. Robert also took great care with his illustrations. He said that his story could have been real, so he wanted his pictures to look real. In his book the year before, he wasn't as concerned with his art work.

Just from these few examples you can see all the skills that each child has been able to develop. I didn't specifically teach my children spelling, vocabulary, composition, how to develop a plot, and so on. But, through reading many, many really good books, they were able to absorb much information and have a good time doing it. Each child is already talking about the books they will write next year. They have also informed me that they want to pick their own topics this time. You see, I'm learning too! Writing books with my children has been the most rewarding thing we have done. It is also a project that can be shared with family and friends and treasured for a lifetime.

INTRODUCTION TO LITERATURE-BASED UNITS

Often you can take a classic, such as *Heidi* or *The Swiss Family Robinson*, and make a complete unit study out of it. Literature-based units are fun and fairly easy to create. It is not necessary for you to completely read the book beforehand. Just glancing through it will give you some ideas of related topics to pursue in the course of your study.

When you begin to plan the unit, there are some pertinent questions you should ask yourself. Where does this story take place? Is this story a true account, based on a true account, or fictional? What character qualities do the individuals in the story possess? (Often you will discover the answer to this question as you read the book with your children.) Is there a biography about the author in print? If not, you can use a reference book at the library such as *Yesterday's Authors of Books for Children* or *The Junior Book of Authors* which will include a few pages about the author. You may photocopy these few pages since the reference books are not available for circulation. Usually an encyclopedia will offer some information about the author, too. Are there any key historical persons mentioned in the book? What about inventions and discoveries pertinent to the time and locale of the story? What other books did the author write? Do they in any way relate to the book you are studying? In what country and time period did the author live?

As you read along, many opportunities will arise which will stimulate areas of interest to investigate. Since you can't be dashing off to the library every other day, an encyclopedia will prove helpful in these instances. For example, if you are reading and you come across a person or place you had not noted earlier, you can look up brief information concerning these topics in the encyclopedia. Most of us don't have time to read the book in its entirety and make elaborate lesson plans ahead of time. It's often these unplanned, spur-of-the-moment interruptions that provide us with the best educational opportunities. I believe it's important to purchase reference materials as opposed to multitudes of textbooks and workbooks. You will get many miles out of reference materials. A new or even old set of encyclopedias may not be feasible for each family to acquire, but I've found a handy reference book which should be in every homeschooling family's library. It is called *A First Dictionary of Cultural Literacy: What Our Children Need to Know*, by E.D. Hirsch, Jr. Families with older students may prefer *The Dictionary of Cultural Literacy: What Every American Needs to Know*, also by Hirsch.

Getting back to our literature-based studies, you will sometimes come across something interesting as you read, such as an invention of the day, unusual animals, various land formations, plants, peoples, battles, bodies of water, political terms, geographical terms, and the list continues. The next time you visit your library you can select books describing some of the more appealing topics. You can keep a list of topics to explore further as you read along. This is also a good activity for the children. As you are reading them a classic, have them compile a list of other topics to investigate. Then have the children look up those particular topics at the library or in an encyclopedia or in another reference book you may own. In this way the children are learning to be observant, and they are participating in the research of the unit study.

Literature-based units are also beneficial in that they provide us with excellent writing models. Many textbooks and workbooks today are written in short, choppy, uninteresting sentences. Classics and other outstanding literary works offer us a feast of literary delicacies. Scenes are vividly described. Characters come alive as the author unveils their personalities. We are able to experience the political, geographical, and economical climate of the story. We learn so many things while being entertained by the author.

This exposure to good literature broadens our vocabulary and our understanding of the world in which we live. Many writing activities naturally flow from this encounter with inspiring literature. Dictate favorite passages to your children noting spelling, punctuation, grammar, vocabulary, and capitalization. Occasionally you might have them rewrite the passage, replacing adjectives with words they choose. Another time they could change the tense or voice of the passage you are studying. Younger children can copy the selections. They might circle words they don't know. They could circle the phonics patterns in the words they do know and tell you how the rules are applied. Other times they could circle all the words with capital letters and explain why these words are capitalized. For more ideas on copying and dictation, I urge you to use the *Learning Language Arts Through Literature* series. After using these books with your children for awhile, you will be able to incorporate many skills into your own unit studies. I really enjoy reading the books myself and getting ideas from them. Since the *Learning Language Arts Through Literature* books incorporate selections from a variety of fine literary works, they contain excellent choices of books for conducting literary units.

The next several pages contain sample literature-based units. Hopefully these will give you some ideas so that you can branch out and conduct a literature-based unit that appeals to your family. Generally, I read the classic aloud to my children. The older children also take turns reading aloud. This gives them good practice with their oral reading skills. If your library has several copies of the classic you have chosen, you may want each reading child to have his or her own copy. Often children like to follow along as they listen. This of course depends on their learning style. Other children, especially younger children do better if they draw while Mom is reading. They can illustrate something from the story.

HEIDI
Author: Johanna Spyri (1827-1901)

For information about the author use a reference book from the library like *Yesterday's Authors of Books for Children*. Often the volume of *Heidi* that you choose will have biographical information at the end of the book. This is the case in the volume that I have chosen of *Heidi* published by Grosset and Dunlap, Inc., the Illustrated Junior Library edition. Read the biographical information before you begin to read the story. As you read the story, see if your children can detect the similarities between Heidi's childhood and the author's childhood. Explain that the author chose to write about things with which she was acquainted. This is helpful to keep in mind as your children compose their own stories. Books originally written in other languages come to us by way of a translation. The volume of *Heidi* that I chose was translated by Helen B. Dole.

Check your library for other books written by Johanna Spyri. My library has a book entitled, *The Children's Christmas Carol*, adapted by Darlene Geis. The Swiss Alps are also the setting for this enchanting tale. This is a good choice for capable children to read on their own or to read to their younger siblings. It helps to reinforce the visual image of the Swiss Alps portrayed in *Heidi*, as well as to further acquaint them with the character of Johanna Spyri.

Setting

The story takes places predominantly in the mountains of Switzerland. Parts of the story take place in Frankfurt, Germany. Obtain library books with information about Switzerland and Germany. Look for books with good pictures so the children can get a glimpse of the vast mountains and beautiful valleys described in *Heidi*. Use maps and a globe to locate Switzerland and Germany. Find out pertinent information about these two countries such as their major exports, religion, education, and government.

As you read with your children, stop at the end of each page or chapter and have them make a list of the words they recall from the story that describe the setting. Have them look for words that describe the scenery, topography, and geographical character of the passages read. What words are used to describe the living quarters? At first you might do this assignment at the end of each page to help your children develop their abilities for locating these descriptive attributes. Later, you can reserve this activity for the end of each chapter. This activity may be oral or written; done on an individual basis or as a group. Are there certain words the author uses frequently? Are her words colorful? As you progress with this word-finding assignment, your children can describe the feelings that are evoked by the author's choice of vocabulary.

Characters

Discuss the characters brought to life in each chapter. Have your children write a list of the phrases used to describe each character. From these descriptions have the children make an illustration of each character. It is not necessary to do this assignment for each chapter. Choose some interesting passages about each chapter to dictate to your children. Discuss punctuation, capitalization, grammar, spelling, and vocabulary. Have the children look up words they cannot define. Have them read the passages inserting their own words for various adjectives. Can they describe the person as accurately or as interestingly as the author can? Does the author use any words that have a different meaning today? If so what are those words?

Bible

Biblical themes are evident throughout the book. In chapter fourteen Heidi relates to the Grandfather the principles of Scripture she learned from the Grandmamma in Frankfurt. She then reads the story of the Prodigal Son to the Grandfather from her beautiful book given to her by the Grandmamma. Realizing that he has been a wayward son, the Grandfather repents and asks the Lord for forgiveness. Read the story of the Prodigal Son with your children and compare the story of the Grandfathers's life with the Biblical story.

Heidi also learned that when we pray, we must pray for the Lord's will to be done in our lives. Often He doesn't answer our prayers immediately because the timing isn't right. He frequently has lessons for us to learn beforehand, and often He has a plan different and better than ours. Heidi's faith is strengthened as these principles become evident in her own life. She learns to trust the Lord in all things and to share her faith with others.

Make a list of the character qualities of the main characters of the story. Using a topical Bible, such as *Nave's Topical Bible*, look up these attributes and read Bible verses pertaining to each character quality. Have your children try to identify which verses go with which individuals. The traits portrayed by the persons in the story may be positive as well as negative.

Narration

Whether oral or written, narration is a great memory building tool. It also helps us to see if our children are not only understanding and retaining the story but if they are improving their vocabulary. If done orally, we can evaluate their progress in verbal presentation. From time to time, we should tape our children giving an oral narration. This will allow them, as well as us, to hear the progress that has taken place. It is easier to compare written narrations, and this should also be done to see if their writing skills have improved.

I find that dinner time is excellent for the children to give oral narrations. They have an audience, including Dad who often cannot be part of the regular studies. This oral narration helps keep him up with the children's studies.

General Information

As mentioned on the preceding pages, the children can make a list of topics that arise as you read. The classic *Heidi* offers many avenues for further research. Switzerland, Germany, mountains, goats, flowers, trees, hymns, physical handicaps, and cheese are just a few. As you read, you will encounter more topics than you could possibly study, so choose to investigate only those of real interest.

To add a little variety to your study of *Heidi* you can check out a book about the famous legendary Swiss hero, William Tell. Several storybook versions exist depicting this gallant individual. In 1829, Gioacchino Rossini's opera, **William Tell** was performed. Today the William Tell Overture is very well known and loved. You may also be able to check out an audio cassette tape or record containing this famous overture.

It is evident from the story that Heidi loved old people, others less fortunate than herself, animals, and nature. Search for evidences of these qualities as you read. These can also be noted in the life of the author as you read biographical information about her.

This beloved classic was written by Johann Wyss. The version we own was published by Grosset and Dunlap Publishers, an Illustrated Junior Library edition. William H.G. Kingston edited this version. This edition was illustrated by Lynd Ward, who also wrote and illustrated the well known book, *The Biggest Bear*.

I found another edition of *The Swiss Family Robinson* at the library. It was complete and unabridged like the one we own, and was also translated by W.H.G. Kingston, but is was published by Children's Press, Chicago. The final section of this edition contains biographical information about the author. Originally the story was written by Pastor John David Wyss who was an expert in farming and nature. He was born in Bern, Switzerland, in 1743. He created this story for his four children and although he recorded it, he filed the papers away. Years after the pastor's death, his son Johann Rudolph Wyss, who was a professor of philosophy at Bern and chief librarian, discovered the manuscript among his father's papers. He made some changes, touched up the story here and there, and took it to a Zurich publisher. It was an immediate success.

The afterword in this version goes on to explain about the translation of the book into French and English. This information is beneficial for understanding how books are translated from one language to another and how we end up with so many different versions of the same story.

Another pleasing feature about this version of *The Swiss Family Robinson* is the informative material located in the margins. Here, difficult words from the text are defined, often accompanied by diagrams, and many of the animals and vegetation mentioned are depicted.

As an interesting activity, you may read a portion from one version of *The Swiss Family Robinson,* and compare it with the same portion from another version. Which translator portrayed a more vivid picture? What other comparisons can you make? Find an abridged version and compare it with an unabridged version. Do they evoke the same feelings? Why or why not?

As in the classic *Heidi*, the predominant characters in *The Swiss Family Robinson* are from Switzerland. The authors of both classics are Swiss. Locate a few library books about Switzerland to enhance your study. Choose books with quality pictures enabling your children to get a glimpse of the incredible geography of Switzerland. You will want to compare the geographical characteristics of Switzerland with the island that the family comes to inhabit.

This book provides an excellent basis for studying character qualities, animals, plants, land formations, geography, and the list multiplies as you read the book. An in depth study of the character qualities of perseverance, determination, patience, ingenuity, faith in the Creator, strong love of family, and hope can be made. Even the first page of this classic gives us a glimpse of the faith of the father, who is also the narrator of the story. We find the family on board ship in the midst of a raging storm.

> *My heart sank as I looked round upon my family in the midst of these horrors. Our four young sons were overpowered by terror. "Dear children," said I, "if the Lord will, He can save us even from this fearful peril; if not, let us calmly yield our lives into His hand, and think of the joy and blessedness of finding ourselves forever and ever united in that happy home above."*

This strong faith in the supreme Creator is carried throughout the book. Chapter one, Shipwrecked and Alone, offers an opportunity to view similar situations documented in Scripture. We read in Acts chapter 27 of Paul sailing for Italy and being caught in a violent wind. A similar event is described in the first chapter of *The Swiss Family Robinson*. Even the wording is very similar. After reading the entire first chapter of the book, read Acts chapter 27 and have your children compare the two accounts. Of course one is a true account and one is not. (One area of contrast is that in the classic, only the Robinson family is spared, and in the Biblical passage, all those on board are spared.) Another Biblical passage that comes to mind when I read this first chapter of the classic is Jonah chapter one. This can also be compared with the account in *The Swiss Family Robinson*. There is also the Biblical account of our Messiah in the storm tossed boats with His disciples in Mark 4:35-41.

As you read chapter one, many areas of interest will surface. For example, they contrived swimming belts for the mother and the boys who could not swim. This provides a good opportunity for discussing the principle of buoyancy. You can experiment by putting various items in a sink of water and finding which ones float and which ones sink. Once again I recommend David Macaulay's, *The Way Things Work*. Many topics such as levers, pulleys, buoyancy, floatation, and friction arise in our story and are simply and concisely addressed in Macaulay's book.

We immediately searched about for what would answer the purpose, and fortunately got hold of a number of empty flasks and tin canister, which we connected two and two together so as to form floats sufficiently buoyant to support a person in the water, and my wife and young sons each willingly put one on.

In the second chapter, A Desolate Island, we begin to see the development of the character of the coast. Have the children begin keeping a list of the descriptions of the land and water. You will encounter terms such as bay and inlet which may require defining. A great number of birds appear in this chapter along with animals on the wrecked ship. The children should make a separate list with the names of these creatures.

As the family was making their way toward the island in their home-made vessel, the dogs were swimming along beside them and growing extremely weary. They occasionally rested their forepaws on the outriggers of the little craft and Jack wished to prevent them from this. The father intervened quoting from the Scriptures, "Stop, that would be unkind as well as foolish; remember, the merciful man regardeth the life of his beast." I looked up merciful in my topical Bible to locate the text for this passage. In **Nave's Topical Bible** it reads as follows. "A righteous man regardeth the life of his beast: but the tender mercies of the wicked are cruel." Proverbs 12:10. (I chose to carry the passage a little further.) You may wish to look up this passage in different versions and compare them. It is interesting because later these dogs serve as not only companions for the family, but as protectors.

Another incident which can be compared with a similar occurrence in Scripture appears in chapter two of the classic.

As soon as we could gather our children around us on dry land, we knelt to offer thanks and praise for our merciful escape, and with full hearts we commended ourselves to God's good keeping for the time to come.

In Genesis 8:20 we find that as soon as Noah was on dry land, he built an altar to the Lord and offered a sacrifice. A comparison can be made also between the animals on Noah's ark and the animals on **The Swiss Family Robinson's** ship. Can your children find any other similarities in the two accounts?

The personalities of the characters in the book become more evident as the story unfolds. Have the children locate a few phrases in each chapter that give evidence of each person's character.

In chapter two we get our first clue as to the whereabouts of the stranded family. Your children may keep a list of clues describing the location of the island.

What kind of information would be useful to collect to make this determination? The scientific explanation below provides a good opportunity to integrate some physical principles of light.

> *The children remarked the suddenness of nightfall, for indeed there had been little or no twilight. This convinced me that we must not be far from the equator, for twilight results from the refraction of the sun's rays. The more obliquely these rays fall, the farther does the partial light extend; while the more perpendicular they strike the earth, the longer do they continue their undiminished force, until, when the sun sinks, they totally disappear, thus producing sudden darkness.*

Have the children copy this passage and make a list of the words they don't understand. Look these words up in a dictionary to help clarify the meaning of the passage. Try creating this phenomenon with a globe or ball and a light. Perhaps the children could then make a diagram to illustrate this experiment.

Chapter three, We Explore Our Island, offers a beautiful illustration made with words. After reading this chapter with your children, re-read some of the more descriptive parts and have them make illustrations to accompany them. They might then copy a few pertinent sentences at the bottom of their pictures.

You will encounter some interesting plant life in this chapter. Keep a list of the plants the Robinson family comes across and the uses they find for them.

Chapter four enables us to study another scientific principle. Fritz watches as his father sucks juice from a sugar cane. He too tries this and finds he cannot extract any juice. A simple library book that leads you through an investigation of the power of air is called, **Simple Science Experiments with Straws**, by Eiji Orii and Masako Orii.

> *"How do you get the juice out, Father?"*
> *"Think a little," I replied. "You are quite as capable as I am of finding out the way, even if you do not know the real reason of your failure."*
>
> *"Oh, of course," said he, "it is like trying to suck marrow from a marrow bone, without making a hole at the other end."*
>
> *"Quite right," I said. "You form a vacuum in your mouth and the end of your tube, and expect the air to force down the liquid from the other end which it cannot possibly enter."*

As you read on, you will find that the coconut milk which Fritz had in his flask had fermented from the heat of the sun. He tugged the cork from his flask and there was a loud pop as the milk came out foaming like champagne. Fritz said it tasted like excellent wine. Read about fermentation from an encyclopedia or library book. Try putting some apple juice or other sweet juice in a jar and setting it in the sun for several hours. What happens? Why?

More animals appear in this chapter. Add them to your list. Have the children relate the account how Fritz adopts a baby monkey. Have one of your children look up monkeys in an encyclopedia or library book, and share some interesting bit of information with the family. Each child can research an animal and relay the findings with the family. Your family may choose to investigate animal classifications and categorize the animals you meet as you read. You can use an encyclopedia or the *Usborne Book of Animal Facts*, by Anita Ganeri. Anita Ganeri and Judy Tatchell wrote another book which you may find helpful called *How to Draw Animals*, published by Usborne. Most library books about animals contain a great deal of evolutionary material. Often the evolutionary content can be overlooked. *Mammals and How They Live*, by Robert M. McClung, is a library book that contains information regarding the way animals are classified.

The *Character Sketches* books, published by Institute in Basic Life Principles, contain interesting information about numerous animals. There are three volumes in the series. Using the indexes found in each volume, you will be able to locate pertinent information about the animals you encounter in your study. These beautifully illustrated books integrate Scripture with the study of nature. They are a delightful addition to any nature study.

In chapter five, We Revisit the Wreck, the children awake to find that Fritz has placed a dead, stiff jackal in a life-like stance before the tent. The other children are quick to try and guess what sort of animal this is. One guesses a yellow dog, another a wolf, and still another a striped fox. The father ends the quarrel by telling them that a jackal partakes of the nature of all three. Using a library book or encyclopedia look up each of these animals, and compare them.

The father and the older boys maneuvered their vessel made of large kegs back to the wrecked ship. Once they arrived they decided to accommodate their craft with equipment suitable for sailing. Here you will find several nautical terms. Look these up under boats or ships in an encyclopedia or book from the library. Some of the terms you will encounter are: mast, sail, spar, lug sail, masthead, rudder, oar, and ballast.

Discuss the plan the father contrived for using flags for signals. Although their system was a simple one, you might want to investigate the signal flags that are used by ships today.

Many domestic animals are mentioned in this chapter. They also have an encounter with a shark. Have one of the children read about sharks and share some interesting information with the family. What category would sharks be classified under?

Now that I have gone through five chapters and given you suggested activities and writing assignments for each, investigate some chapters on your own.

I would like to make a few suggestions for writing assignments that you can integrate as you choose. You may select a sentence or paragraph from each chapter that you feel emphasizes the most valuable character qualities. Have your children copy these selections or take them from dictation. Using a topical Bible you can investigate what the Bible has to say about the various character traits.

Choose a paragraph that is very descriptive. Have your children look up those descriptive words in a thesaurus, and re-write the paragraph substituting the new words. Discuss the feeling evoked by this change. Is the message as clear? (Often a thesaurus can be checked out of the library.)

Many difficult words appear in the text. Their meanings, however, can generally be discerned through context. Choose a couple of sentences with complicated words. Have the children verbally replace these words with words from their own vocabulary as they are able to discern the unfamiliar words from context. Later try this as a written exercise and have the children copy the sentences, omitting the unfamiliar words and leaving a blank in their place. Then have them fill in their own words.

Don't try to define every difficult word as you read to your children. This causes reading to be choppy and uninteresting. A few exercises involving unfamiliar words from time to time will be far more beneficial.

I'm just going to touch on some of the remaining chapters of the book. Chapter seven, We Build a Bridge, exemplifies some engineering principles as they seek a way to complete their task. In chapter eight, The Journey to the Wonderful Trees, we find that these magnificent trees are fig-bearing mangroves of the Antilles. Locate a book on trees for an accurate description and illustration. What were some of the peculiarities of the trees mentioned in the chapter? What new animal appears and how does it prove useful to the family?

In the next chapter, The Tree-House, we find the father using geometry to aid in the task of constructing a ladder of proper height to reach a desired branch.

"Geometry will simplify the operation considerably; with its help the altitude of the highest mountains are ascertained. We may, therefore, easily find the height of the branch."

The following passage offers an explanation for determining unknown heights by similar triangles. The triangle EBA is similar to the triangle EDC because angle E is the same in both triangles and the angle ABE and angle CDE, by construction are both right angles. Therefore this equality results:

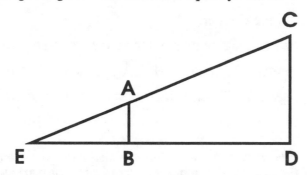

Thales, a mathematician of Ancient Greece, surprised the Egyptians when he was able to tell them the height of their Great Pyramid. By comparing the shadow of his staff to the height of the staff and the shadow of the pyramid to the height of the pyramid, he was able to find the height very quickly. He was using this same principle of similar triangles.

The father also constructs a bow and arrow. Most boys are interested in bows and arrows. You may wish to find a library book about archery. This is a sport that my boys really enjoy. Read Psalms 127:3-5.

A Visit to Tentholm, chapter 10, begins with the father quoting from Scripture:

> "`Six days shalt thou labor and do all that thou hast to do, but on the seventh, thou shalt do no manner of work.' This is the seventh day," I replied, "on it, therefore, let us rest." "The leafy shade of this great tree is far more beautiful than any church," I said; "there will we worship our Creator."

These passages and the dialogue that goes along with them, offer good material for discussion. Read the Genesis account of creation noting what the Lord has said about the seventh day. It is interesting that the father realized that they did not need a church to worship the Creator. What is the church?

As you read, you will find that the family gave names to their various abodes and bodies of water on the island. Can the children recall all the names? Maybe your children will want to re-name some of the landmarks, bodies of water, buildings, and parks in your area. Perhaps they can think of names that would be significant to them. (If you have read the Anne of Green Gables series, you will find that Anne always made up names for various places in her town. She felt the original names lacked imagination.)

There are 44 chapters in all. Therefore, I could not possibly discuss them all in this book. You will encounter many forms of plant and animal life which you can investigate and classify. You will read about many ingenious devices which the family contrives to make their life more agreeable. You will experience their family unity and dependence on the Creator.

One last activity I would like to mention is to encourage your children to keep a simple log or journal. Buying or making a special book to record life's daily happenings will prove helpful. Chapter nineteen supplies us with an encouragement in this endeavor.

> *In the evening, when our room was illuminated with wax candles, I wrote a journal of all the events, which had occurred since our arrival in this foreign land. And, while the mother was busy with her needle and Ernest was making sketches of birds, beasts and flowers with which he had met during the past months, Fritz and Jack taught little Franz to read.*

THE PLANT SITTER
A Literature-based Unit for the Early Grades

The Plant Sitter, by Gene Zion and illustrated by Margaret Bloy Graham, is a charming story written in 1959. The book centers around a young boy, Tommy, who begins a plant sitting business to occupy his summer days. His father says he's too busy to take a vacation this year, so Tommy makes valuable use of his free time by caring for his neighbors' plants while they are away for the summer. He earns two cents a day for each plant he tends. Tommy trots away with his wagon to gather the neighbors' plants, and soon his house is overflowing with greenery. The plants continue to flourish under Tommy's care and they seem to almost engulf the house. One night, Tommy has a dream that the plants destroy his house. The next day he rushes to the library to do some research on plants. Following the advice he finds in the library books, Tommy increases his plant business. Soon the neighbors return and are very pleased with the condition of their plants. Then Tommy gets a real reward. His father, who constantly grumbled that the plants were a nuisance, now realizes he misses the plants. Therefore, he decides the family should take a trip to the country.

About the Author and Illustrator

Gene Zion has written a number of books for children including: *Harry the Dirty Dog, Dear Garbage Man, No Roses for Harry*, and several others. Margaret Bloy Graham illustrated these books as well as *The Plant Sitter*. Your children will probably enjoy these stories too.

Library Books

Drawing From Nature, by Jim Arnosky, contains a very informative section on drawing plants. The text, as well as the illustrations, gives insight into creating life-like images. *Linnea's Windowsill Garden*, by Chritina Bjork and Lena Anderson, is a terrific little book filled with fascinating facts and fun projects. It includes a section about making cuttings. You will find this handy information because Tommy makes cuttings from his neighbor's plants in *The Plant Sitter*. (He did this to prevent his house from being strangled by the plants!) *Linnea's Windowsill Garden* also gives a brief but interesting explanation for the Latin names for plants. *A First Look at Leaves*, by Millicent E. Selsam. This is a great book to help you and your children discover the many different characteristics of leaves. It also includes a section on making leaf prints. *Usborne First Nature Flowers*, by Rosamun K. Cox and Barbara Cork, includes a good explanation about pollination. (Keep this simple with younger children.) *Plant Families*, by Carol Lerner, is an examination of twelve of the world's largest and most familiar plant families. *Hands on Science: Seeds to Plants*, by Dr. Jeffery Bates has colorfully illustrated text offering basic information about topics including seeds, germination, roots, stems, leaves, buds and twigs, flowers, fruits, and classifications. (Best if used primarily for its illustrations.) *The Young Scientist Investigates Seeds and Seedlings*, by Terry Jennings is a good choice to read aloud to your children. It offers an introduction to seeds and seedlings without using complicated terms. Several art projects and simple experiments are included. *Anna's Garden Songs*, and *Anna's Summer Songs*, by Lena Anderson include poems about vegetables, trees, flowers, ferns, and fruits depicted in charming pictures. *Linnea in Monet's Garden*, also by Lena Anderson, (this is the same Linnea who has a windowsill garden listed above) offers a look at fine art as it encompasses nature. *The Random House Book of Poetry for Children*, selected by Jack Prelutsky. Using the subject index, look up "flowers and plants" and you will find a listing of related poems. *Seeds and More Seeds*, by Millicent Selsam, is an "I Can Read" book. *Little Owl and the Weed*, by Constance Boyle. *The Tiny Seed*, by Eric Carle, tells the fascinating story of the life cycle of a flower using colorful collage illustrations. Robert Quackenbush makes use of his unique storytelling abilities and kid-appealing illustrations to bring to life Luther Burbank, the world famous plant breeder in *Here a Plant, There a Plant, Everywhere a Plant, Plant!: A Story of Luther Burbank*. *Cactus,* by Cynthia Overbeck, contains color photographs depicting the great variety of shapes and sizes in the cactus family. (If you cannot locate this book, find a colorful book about cactus plants.) *An Eyewitness Book: Plants,* like most of the books in the Eyewitness Series is well written and includes terrific photographs.

You will want to read *The Plant Sitter* with your children several times during the course of your unit study. If you have a child who is able, have him read aloud portions of the story after you have read them aloud at least once. If the child is just learning to read, it's best if he is familiar with the story before he attempts to read it himself. He will not be pre-occupied with trying to follow the story line as well as trying to decipher each word. This is why I advocate that a beginning reader dictate a story to his mom or dad and then read it, or a portion of it, out loud. His familiarity with the story will allow him to coast over the more difficult words. His self-confidence will be boosted and much real learning will take place.

I believe *The Plant Sitter* is especially appealing to young children. Tommy, the star of the show, is a young boy who uses his initiative to start a productive business.

Bible

There are a multitude of references to plants in the Bible, and because this unit is designed primarily for young children, I will not even try to hit every allusion to plants. Remember, it's best to keep a unit simple. More in depth studies can be made at a future date. It is not important that your child learn everything there is to know about plants at this time. It is not even important that they learn the normal information about plants that is expected for their age level. Most of what is written in textbooks for young children on this topic consists of phrases like, Plants are nice. Plants have leaves. Plants are green. Plants help us. Most two year olds have figured this out for themselves. Let's put away the "twaddle" and let our children get on with real learning.

I used *Nave's Topical Bible* and *The Biblical Cyclopedia Index* found in *The Open Bible, New American Standard, Expanded Edition.* To begin our study, let's go back to the beginning. I suggest reading the first chapter of Genesis with your children, focusing on Genesis 1:11-13. (NAS)

> *Then God said, "Let the earth sprout vegetation, plants yielding seed, and fruit trees bearing fruit after their kind, with seed in them, on the earth;" and it was so. And the earth brought forth vegetation, plants yielding seed after their kind, and trees bearing fruit, with seed in them, after their kind; and God saw that it was good. And there was evening and morning a third day.*

Genesis 1:29-30 (NAS)

> *Then God said, "Behold, I have given you every plant yielding seed that is on the surface of all the earth, and every tree which has fruit yielding seed; it shall be food for you; and to every beast of the earth, and to every bird of the sky and to every thing that moves on the earth which has life, I have given every green plant for food;" and it was so.*

Discuss words with your children such as seed, fruit, kind, yielding, sprout, vegetation, and bearing. Note that the plants were created on the third day. Ask your children why they think that the Lord created plants on the third day. When were the animals created? When was man created?

Another interesting passage to study and perhaps even memorize is the first Psalm. A variety of plants are found in the Bible. Although it would be tedious to look them all up, I have listed some that you may want to investigate.

Aloe	Psalm 45:8, Prov. 7:17
Bramble	Judges 9:14, 15
Brier	Judges 8:7,16
Broom ("Juniper")	Psalm 120:4
Calamus	Song of Solomon 4:14
Camphire ("Henna")	Song of Solomon 1:14
Crocus	Isaiah 35:1
Cummin	Isaiah 28, 25, 17
Dill	Matthew 23:23
Garlic	Numbers 11:5
Gourd	2 Kings 4:39
Grass	Psalm 103:15
Hyssop	Exodus 12:22
Lily	Song of Solomon 5:13
Mallows	Job 30:4
Mandrakes	Genesis 30:14-16
Mint	Matthew 23:23
Mustard	Matthew 13:31
Myrtle	Isaiah 55:13
Nard	Song of Solomon 4:13, 14
Rue	Luke 11:42
Saffron	Song of Solomon 4:13, 14
Spelt	Ezekiel 4:9
Thorn	Judges 8:7
Vine of Sodom	Deuteronomy 32:32
Wormwood	Deuteronomy 29:18
Wheat	Matthew 13:25, Luke 16:7

Using *Nave's Topical Bible*, look under botany to find a listing of many other plants found in the Bible. It is interesting to note the Lord's laws concerning hybridization. See Leviticus 19:19 and Deuteronomy 22:9-11. Hybrid plant and animals are sterile and frustrate the purpose of creation. Note that in Genesis the Lord created the plants yielding seed and the fruit trees bearing fruit after their kind. Through hybridization, man seeks to improve on the Divine Creator's work. Quoting from *The Institutes of Biblical Law*, by Rousas John Rushdoony:

> *"Knowledge and science require a basis of law, fixity, and pattern. With out this there can be neither science nor progress. Hybridization is an attempt to deny the validity of law. Its penalty is an enforced sterility. In every area, where man seeks potentiality by a denial of God's law, the penalty remains the same, limited gains and long-range sterility."*

As you read the biography of Luther Burbank, you will see why many religious and civic groups were appalled when he published his catalog entitled, "New Creations in Fruits and Flowers." I suggest reading Luther Burbank's biography by Robert Quackenbush at this time. Another interesting avenue to explore is grafting. Grafting is different from hybridization. Look up both grafting and hybridization in your dictionary. For a Biblical analogy to grafting, read Matthew 11:17-24. It is interesting to note that an olive tree was grafted into another olive tree, it was not grafted into a peach tree or an almond tree.

Activities

Have your children make a list of all the different kinds of plants they can name. It may be helpful to write each letter of the alphabet down the side of your paper and have them think of a plant name for each letter. This is a good activity to do as a group. Older children may want to try this activity on their own. In conducting this study, I find that I know the names of a very limited number of plants. I feel ignorant when people, generally older people, can rattle off the names of hundreds of plants. Charlotte Mason in her book *Home Education* states that this familiarity with nature used to be common among people. Somehow we have lost this bond with our Heavenly Father's creation, but you and your children have the opportunity to recapture it. Take frequent nature hikes and invest in a good field guide for plant identification purposes.

Supply each child with a paper sack to begin your nature hike. We have an alley behind our house which abounds with interesting vines, weeds, acorns, pine cones, twigs, and blossoming beauties. (You know, dandelions, buttercups, and so forth.) Allow each child to fill his sack, encouraging each to find leaves and stems that look interesting, not necessarily pretty. When you arrive home, spread a table with newspapers and empty the sacks on the papers. Ask the children to draw the specimens of their choice. They may want to draw any bugs that sneaked in too! Using a field guide, you may be able to identify most of the specimens that your children have collected. A review of the book *Drawing From Nature* will give you and your children some hints about drawing plant life. Discuss the various leaf formations, stems, roots, and so on. *A First Look at Leaves* is a great book to read with your children at this time. Try classifying the specimens gathered according to their leaves. For example, group the plants together that have leaves with smooth edges, wavy edges, or edges like a saw. Discuss symmetry found in nature. A useful library book pertaining to this is *Symmetry*, by Ed Emberly. Leaf prints are fun to make. Follow the directions given in *A First Look at Leaves*. I have included brief instructions in case this library book is not available to you.

How to Make Leaf Prints

Materials: ink roller, printing ink, printing paper, magazine with a slick cover, tweezers, leaves, newspapers.

Spread the newspapers on a table. Lay the magazine on the newspapers and squeeze a generous amount of ink on the slick surface of the magazine. Spread the ink on the roller. Place a leaf on a clean piece of paper and spread the ink on the smooth side of the leaf. Carefully lift the leaf with the tweezers and lay it face down on the printing paper. Place a clean piece of paper over the leaf and rub it gently with your hand, being careful not to move the leaf. Remove the top paper and the leaf to expose your beautiful leaf print. You might like to try pressing leaves too. My son Raymond pressed a bug once, and he decided never to do that again!

Perhaps your children will want to compose a poem about some of the specimens they gathered. Read some of the poems from **The Random House Book of Poetry for Children**. (Use the subject index to locate poems about flowers and plants.) We particularly liked "Old Quin Queeribus," by Nancy Byrd Turner; and "Wild Flowers," by Peter Newel. **Anna's Garden Songs** and **Anna's Summer Songs** are both full of delightful poems about plants. Encourage your children to use the words they have chosen in describing their nature specimens to write a poem. It is often helpful to make a list of any words that relate to your topic; for instance the descriptive words about the specimens, and then find words to rhyme with them.

Now is a good time to read **The Plant Sitter** again with your children. Have your children list some of the ways that Tommy took care of his plants. Have the children copy the portions of the book that explain how Tommy cared for the plants. If your child needs help with proper letter formation, write out the selections for him neatly. I suggest you write one line and then skip a line. This enables your child to write directly under the words you have written. You might want to have capable children write the passages as you dictate them. You will find that two key elements are water and sunlight. Using a library book about plants, read selections pertaining to these topics. **Linneas's Windowsill Garden** contains informative sections that will prove helpful such as The Art of Watering, The Water Cycle, My Own Little Water Cycle, and What do Plants Need to Survive?

We noted that Tommy gave the cactus plants very little water. I chose a library book on cactus plants and read significant portions that explained why they need so little water. The pictures were interesting also. Tommy did some research at the library and found that he could make cuttings from the plants, and that these cuttings would grow into new plants. *Linnea's Windowsill Garden* contains a section entitled, "Here's How You Make a Cutting." This book is loaded with easy projects for your children to enjoy. Help your children keep a log of their plant experiments. List the materials needed, procedure followed, and a daily record of their observations. I advise that they make sketches to accompany their journals.

If interested, you may expand your study to include flowers, pollination, fruit and seeds, germination, roots, shoots and so on. I suggest reading *The Young Scientist Investigates: Seeds and Seedlings*, by Terry Jennings. Don't overextend yourself on this unit, but make it fun and interesting. Use the additional library books recommended, or others you may find, to enhance your study, not to complicate it.

Read some of the story books about plants that I listed in the library section. Allow capable children to read aloud from these books. Perhaps your children will want to write a book of their own about plants. Shape books are an excellent choice for this unit.

If you care to take a closer look at fine art, read *Linnea in Monet's Garden*. Claude Monet was an impressionistic artist. Much of his work focused on the elements of his garden at Giverny. Using the subject card catalog in the fine arts section, look up plants and flowers. This resource will direct you to a variety of artists' works pertaining to your unit. Select a few books with reproductions of art that include interesting plants and/or flowers. Allow your children to look at a picture for one minute and then tell you as many things as they can remember about the picture. Then have them look at the same picture again to make more observations. This activity helps to strengthen their observation skills. If your children like to draw or paint, they might like to copy a favorite botanical painting.

SCIENCE

AVIATION UNIT

The study of aviation can be broken into several basic categories. I have chosen to focus on the history of aviation, and the elements of flight, which includes the workings of a plane and the effects of air and weather in aviation.

Library Books and Other Materials Pertaining to the History of Aviation

The Smithsonian Book of Flight for Young People, by Walter J. Boyne. The photographs in this book are outstanding. Choose sections from this book to read to your children, particularly Part 1, From Dream to Reality. This section gives a good overview of the history of aviation. An older child may wish to do further reading in the book, but the text is quite extensive. *Flying Machine, An Eyewitness Book*, by Andrew Nahum. A photo essay outlining the history and development of aircraft from hot-air balloons to jetliners. Includes information on the principles of flight and the inner workings of a variety of flying machines. *History of Flight Coloring Book*, by A.G. Smith, published by Dover. *The First Flight, The Story of the Wright Brothers*, by Richard Taylor. *Amelia Earhart Takes Off*, by Fern G. Brown. Another biography is *The Story of Amelia Earhart, Lost*, by Patricia Lauber. *Clear the Cow Pasture, I'm Coming in For A Landing! A Story of Amelia Earhart*, by Robert Quackenbush. *The Glorious Flight, Across the Channel by Louis Bleriot*, by Alice and Martin Provensen. *The Glorious Flight* won the Caldecott Medal for the most distinguished American picture book for children published in 1983. *The Flight of the Lone Eagle, Charles Lindbergh Flies Nonstop from New York to Paris*, by John T. Foster. A more detailed biography is *Charles Lindbergh*, by Blythe Randolph. *The Way Things Work*, by David Macaulay. Includes easy to understand explanations of flight, the airplane, flying machines, an airliner wing, the helicopter, the jump jet, the hydrofoil, the jet engine, the rocket engine and more.

Library Books and Other Materials Pertaining to the Elements of Flight

The Old Fashioned Paper Airplane Book, published by Common Sense Press. *The Great Paper Airplane Book*, by Seymour Simpson. Shows how to design and make a variety of paper airplanes, and explains the science of flight. *The Airplane and How It Works*, by David I. Urquhart. The author explains in a simple manner what makes an airplane fly and the forces that act on a plane in flight. *Flying*, by Gail Gibbons. Gail Gibbons has provided an easy-reader-type book about aircraft. ***Experimenting With Air and Flight***, by Ormiston H. Walker. Using examples found in nature and presenting experiments you can perform, the author guides you through the basic principles of aerodynamics. You will investigate the properties of air and the four forces at work on an aircraft in motion: lift, thrust, drag, and gravity. ***How Birds Fly***, by Russell Freedman. ***The Miracle of Flight***, by Richard Cromer. ***Feathers Plain and Fancy***, by Hilda Simon. ***Simple Weather Experiments With Everyday Materials***, by Muriel Mandell. ***The Cloud Book***, by Brian Cosgrove. Photographs and text depict different aspects of weather. ***Weather Words and What They Mean***, by Gail Gibbons. Another easy-reader-type book. ***Amazing Air, Science Club***, by Henry Smith. Contains experiments relating to the forces of air. ***Weather Forecasting***, by Gail Gibbons.

Other Library Books

Why Can't I Fly?, by Ken Brown. A picture book about an ostrich that wants to fly. ***Amelia's Flying Machine***, by Barbara Shook Hazen. A true story from the life of Amelia Earhart.

The History of Aviation

I suggest reading a couple of the biographies mentioned previously to help your children get a feel for the circumstances surrounding the early years of aviation. You may want to choose biographies of other pertinent individuals such as Eddie Rickenbacker, Richard Byrd, James "Jimmy" Doolittle, and Charles "Chuck" Yeager. Several of the books mentioned provide a brief overview of the history of aviation which will prove beneficial. Of course, it would be difficult to read biographies about everyone who played a part in aviation's past.

As you read, note the ideas of flying expressed by early man in mythology and legend. For example, research the Greek god Hermes. Read about Pegasus, Phaeton, Daedalus and Icarus, Sinbad the sailor and his Roc, Arabs and their flying carpets. Others to include are Simon, a Roman magician who tried to fly from a tower, and Wan-Hoo, the Chinese ruler who attached 47 large rockets to his chair to fly to the moon. Compare ancient myths and legends about flight to modern tales about space creatures. What happens when people reject the knowledge of a Divine Creator? They are left to devise their own explanations of man and the universe. Observe early designs for flying machines such as those of Da Vinci, early gliders, balloons, and all types of powered aircraft from the Wright brothers to modern times.

Investigate the Japanese custom of flying kites to celebrate children's growth. Obtain a library book about kite making and create your own kite. Discuss the principles of aerodynamics that come into play. How does a tail help a kite? Does it correspond to any part of an airplane? A terrific library book about kites for young children is *Catch the Wind!: All About Kites*, by Gail Gibbons.

Read the poem, "Darius Green and His Flying Machine" by John T. Trowbridge, from *Best Loved Poems*, by Garden City Publishers, NY. If you cannot locate that particular poetry volume, look for *The Oxford Book of American Light Verse*, chosen and edited by William Harmon. I found this in the reference section and photocopied the poem. (Be sure to have plenty of change for the copy machine as the poem is about five pages long!) Discuss the poem noting examples of cause and effect relationships, clues to time and location, and foreshadowing of later events.

Check out video tapes relative to your study. Compare the information given in these tapes with the information you have read.

Read about and discuss the parts of an airplane and their functions: wing, fuselage, tail assembly and landing gear. Construct a model airplane and identify the plane's basic parts. (*Making Model Aircraft*, by Bryan Philpott.) Use an atlas to locate the latitude and longitude of five cities. Read a library book about the magnetic compass with your children. Discuss and examine the pocket compass that hikers use. Learn about the differences between magnetic north and true north. Construct a simple, working compass. Investigate aeronautical charts, the altimeter, the tachometer, time in aviation, and the airspeed indicator, using an encyclopedia or library book. Read about internal combustion engines and jet engines. You will find David Macaulay's *The Way Things Work* helpful for finding much of the information. The ages of your children and the amount of information you want to cover will dictate how in depth your study will be. Some of the more complicated topics can be further investigated at a later date.

Conduct several experiments that show the properties of air. *Experimenting With Air and Flight* is an excellent book. It includes experiments investigating such topics as: Is Air Real?, Air Pressure and the Power of Air, Wing Shapes, Drag and Streamlining, Finding the Best Shape, Thrust, Propellers and Helicopters, Autogyros, Jets and Jet Engines, How Birds Fly, Speed and Balance, Birds and Insects, Gliders, Parachutes, Detecting Air Currents, Measuring Airspeed, Wind Tunnels, Outdoor Observation with Plants, Balloons, Rocket Propulsion, Into Orbit, Weightlessness, and more. Have the children keep a notebook describing their experiments, noting procedures and observations.

Atmospheric conditions have a great influence on aviation. Weather and climate conditions must be carefully observed. Using books you have chosen from the library, investigate the basic causes of weather. Study about atmospheric pressure, wind, temperature, humidity, dew, frost and clouds. The nature of clouds is determined by temperature, turbulence, foreign particles and water vapor content. Have your children keep a weather calendar during the course of your study. Design symbols to represent sunny, cloudy, rainy, or snowy conditions. Record variations in weather during the day. Note cloud formations as well. What types of clouds are visible? Note the degree of visibility: haze, fog, rain, etc. Not the forces of wind. High winds mean there will be a change in weather conditions. Using a weather experiment library book, make a chemical hygrometer to show the moisture content in the atmosphere. Measure precipitation. Record temperature. You will find several pertinent experiments in the book, *Simple Weather Experiments With Everyday Materials*. There are a variety of weather experiment books available.

Additional Activities

Visit an airport. Make a timeline depicting aviation history. Have the children draw or trace pictures to go on this timeline. Investigate careers in aviation. Discuss the uses of the general aviation airplane: battling forest fires, reforesting clearcut areas, law enforcement, highway traffic control, planting crops, fertilizing crops, studying wildlife, feeding livestock, detecting plant disease by use of infrared photography, commuter airlines, mail operations, banking operations, business flying, sport flying, etc.

Have your children write to the:

> Department of Transportation
> Federal Aviation Administration
> Washington, DC 20591

or to:

> Beachcraft Aircraft Corporation
> Wichita, Kansas 67201

Many writing activities can be integrated into this unit. Have the children copy or take from dictation significant information. Keep a list of aviation terms and their meanings as you encounter them in your reading.

There is a lot of material available on this unit of study. Don't get bogged down trying to integrate too many subjects into this study. I specifically wrote a separate unit on birds because it is too tedious to study birds and aviation at the same time. The library books regarding aviation should offer enough material concerning birds for the present time. At a later date you may wish to study birds in more detail. At that time, you may briefly review some of the points of aviation.

Integrate music, poetry, and art as it suits your needs. Listen to a tape of "The Flight of the Bumble Bee". Your children can write a paragraph about how this music makes them feel. Can your children write a poem about the history of aviation? For a challenging activity, write a group of poems utilizing the aviation terms your children have compiled. Have each child draw pictures of his favorite aircraft. This can include some of the early forms of aircraft to supersonic jets.

Bible

Since weather plays a vital role in aviation, we can investigate the properties of weather found in the Bible. Using a concordance, you can look up wind and find a number of passages. *Nave's Topical Bible* has a listing for weather. It suggests Matthew 16:2,3. I want to also include Matthew 16:1.

> *And the Pharisees and Sadducees came up, and testing Him asked Him to show them a sign from heaven. But He answered and said to them, "When it is evening, you say, 'It will be fair weather, for the sky is red.' And in the morning, 'There will be a storm today, for the sky is red and threatening.' So you know how to discern the appearance of the sky, but cannot discern the signs of the times?" (NASV)*

You will also find Job chapter 37 to be interesting as well as chapter 38. These give reference to our Maker's mighty power over the elements of the world. Discuss the importance of the verses mentioned and how we should respond to man's forecasting.

ASTRONOMY UNIT

Videos

Look for videos on space and space exploration in your public library and video rental stores.

Books

Astronomy and the Bible, Questions and Answers, by Donald B. De Young. This book is a great resource, as many of the library books present a humanistic view of the solar system. Another valuable resource for this unit is *Pocket Science: The Solar System*, published by Ideal. Instructions are included for making models of the planets, and experiments are outlined to acquaint children with the surfaces of the planets. Crossword and word puzzles are included as well.

Library Books

Find the Constellations, by H.A. Rey. My children really liked this book. It was always disappearing from the school room! *Ancient Astronomy*, by Isaac Asimov. *Space Songs* and also *Sky Songs*, by Myra Cohn Livingston, poet; Leonard E. Fisher, painter. *Worlds Beyond: The Art of Chesley Bonestell*, by Frederick C. Durant, III and Ron Miller. Bonestell desired to accurately depict the planets of the solar system. He said he was disillusioned by artists' conceptions of the planets. Many of these incredible paintings date from the 1940's. (This book is located in the fine arts section of the library.) You may want to choose a simple book on telescopes. David Macaulay's book, *The Way Things Work*, is an excellent choice for brief information about telescopes. It also contains material on space telescopes, space probes, and satellites. You will find a multitude of books on astronomy in the youth section as well as the adult section of the library.

Bible

Use a concordance and look up words like star, constellation, heavens, moon, sun, and so on. If you have a topical Bible, like *Nave's Topical Bible*, you can look up astronomy and it will lead you to many passages which you might not find using a concordance. These passages make great selections for the children to type or copy. The Genesis account of creation is very appropriate to study at this time. You will also find the book previously mentioned, *Astronomy and the Bible*, to be a tremendous resource. As your children copy or type these passages, have them make a list of the words that pertain to your study. This is a good time to teach them how to use a topical Bible and a concordance.

Projects

I don't like to get hung up on a lot of projects, but this unit begs for one. Use the **Pocket Science** listed above or a library book that has instructions for creating a mobile of the solar system. You can use styrofoam balls, or balloons and papier-maché. We chose the messier papier-maché version. I read to the children about the different planets as they constructed their models.

This is also a good unit for conducting experiments pertaining to light. Buy some solar paper from a school supply store for some interesting fun with sunlight.

Arts

Using the library books listed above (if they are available), have your children paint or draw space scapes. Pastels done on rough paper give a nice effect. *Space Songs* and *Sky Songs* have very interesting pictures, and Chesley Bonestell's paintings are extremely appealing. The library usually has a number of books with instructions on making a variety of spacecraft. My boys enjoy those craft books.

History

I suggest you read two or three biographies of famous astronomers. It's helpful if you read them in chronological order, as most astronomers based their research on the findings of earlier astronomers. I have listed some astronomers, but I am not giving specific titles of individuals mentioned. These can easily be located in the junior biography section of your public library. Choose simple or more complicated biographies as suits your needs.

Aristarchus: 3rd century B.C., Greek astronomer.

Aristole: 384-322 B.C., Greek philosopher and natural scientist.

Ptolemy: 2nd Century A.D., Egyptian astronomer.

Nicolaus Copernicus: 1473-1543, Polish astronomer and doctor.

Tycho Brahe: 1546-1601, Danish astronomer.

Galileo Galilei: 1546-1642, Italian physicist, mathematician.

Johannes Kepler: 1571-1630, German mathematician and astronomer, assistant to Brahe.

Isaac Newton: 1642-1727, scientist whose discoveries were based on the work of Copernicus, Galileo, Brahe, and Kepler.

Isaac Asimov's ***Ancient Astronomy*** gives a brief account of the works and beliefs of many of these early astronomers. You may also be interested in studying about space exploration. You could read a biography of Neil Armstrong.

Language Arts

Read ***Space Songs*** or ***Sky Songs***, or other books with poems about the sun, moon, planets, comets, etc. Have your children copy selected poems or take them from dictation. In the two books mentioned above, the poems are printed in various ways so as to create an appropriate design. If these books are not available to you, choose a large poetry volume with a subject index and look up words pertinent to your study. You should be able to find a number of poems relating to our solar system. Read information about the planets, sun, moon, stars, asteroids, comets, etc. (For this use library books, ***Pocket Science*** sheets, or ***Astronomy and the Bible***.) Have your children make a list of significant words relating to each category. They can compile these lists as you proceed through the unit study. After their lists are finished, have your children use them to write space poems. They may choose to write about one planet, comets, the moon, or the solar system in general. It is helpful for them to make a list of words that rhyme with the words they have already listed. You may choose to introduce several forms of poetry, such as Haiku, a Japanese form of poetry usually dealing with nature. It contains seventeen syllables in lines of 5, 7, and 5 syllables. This type of poetry does not usually rhyme.

You can think of many language arts assignments for this unit. Sometimes you may have your children copy or take dictation information about the planets or other relative topics. For younger children, dictate simple sentences from the books you read, and discuss the phonics rules in the words they have written. Have your children illustrate the passages they write. Your children may want to write a fictional story about space travel and utilize facts about our universe. You can explain that many authors write fictional stories that take place in real places and historical time periods. You might also discuss science fiction. Another fun activity is to make an A to Z listing of terms relating to astronomy and the solar system.

ANTS UNIT

Books

If you own or have access to any of the *Character Sketches* books published by the Institute in Basic Life Principles, use the indexes found in these books to locate interesting information concerning ants. (Ordering information is included in the reference section.)

Library Books

An Ant Colony, by Fischer-Nagel. *Ladis and the Ant*, by Sanchez-Silva. *The Ants Go Marching*, by B. Freschet. *Ant Cities*, by Arthur Dorros. *Ants*, by Yazima. *The Visit*, by Diane Wolkstein. *The Random House Book of Poetry for Children. Hidden Messages*, by Van Woerkom. *Two Bad Ants*, by Chris Van Allsburg. (This book was a favorite of mine. It is predominantly a picture book, but it is hilarious. It also offers a good opportunity to discuss the consequences of disobedience.) You will probably find many books on ants, so pick a few that look interesting.

Terminology

Have your children keep a record of terms and their meanings as you encounter them in your reading. They should also make a diagram of an ant and list the body parts.

Activities

My mother bought the children an ant farm and we stocked it with ants from the park behind our house. You can get ants through the mail, but you cannot get queen ants because they are protected by law. We raided a large ant bed (red ants) and were able to get many queens. Some of the ants were in the larvae and pupae stage. They were fascinating to watch. (We did get bit trying to get them in the farm! Wear gloves. We also roasted our ants by placing them in a window with a sunny exposure. Try not to do that.) The children took turns feeding and watering the ants. It is a good idea to keep a record of the ants' activities. This can be done in a simple manner, and it teaches the children observation skills.

Games

My children each made an ant colony game. I gave them simple books about ants and had them make up 25 questions and answers pertaining to ants. This activity was very educational as they learned to read to locate specific information. They also had to put this information in the form of a question. They used index cards to write the questions, and the answers were included on the bottom of each card. My daughter Michelle typed all her question cards and used color coding dots (used for coding files) to indicate specific categories. The children made "event cards" as well as factual cards. These cards helped to liven up the game. For example, one of my children's cards read: "You forgot to pick up the Queen's gown at the Royal Ant Dry Cleaners. Go back 4 spaces." The children made game boards out of poster board. Underground ant tunnels and rooms served as excellent game routes. They made ant playing pieces out of styrofoam pieces used for packaging material. The children also wrote their own game rules. The older girls typed their rules while the younger boys dictated theirs to me. It is a good idea to play several kinds of games before the children devise their own game. This game making was a lot of fun. We spent a week making the games.

Bible

Proverbs 6:6-8; 30:25. It is interesting that the Lord uses something as simple as ants to convey His principles. As you read, you will find there are over 10,000 different kinds of ants. This is an excellent opportunity to discuss the complexity of creation. Each kind of ant was designed for a special purpose. We are much more precious to our Heavenly Father than the ants. He created each of us for a special purpose also.

Language Arts

I dictated passages about ants to the older children. The younger children copied sentences I chose pertaining to ants. These selections were taken from library books and *Character Sketches*. As the children did these writing exercises, we discussed punctuation, capitalization, vocabulary, spelling, nouns, verbs, and adjectives. We also read a number of poems about ants. *The Random House Book of Poetry for Children* has two funny poems: "Ants, Although Admirable, Are Awfully Aggravating" and "The Ant Olympics." The first poem offered a good opportunity to discuss alliteration. After brainstorming words relating to ants, the children wrote their own ant poems and illustrated them. The older children typed their poems.

Most people think of John James Audubon, the American woodsman, when they think of birds. He was probably the greatest American naturalist and obviously the greatest of all bird painters. He traveled the frontier country of America and painted birds in their natural habitats. He was born April 26, 1785.

As I began to look for books about birds in my public library, I found them in three basic areas. First, in the children's section I found factual books pertaining to birds. Then I located poetry books with various poems about birds. Next I looked for a biography of Audubon. I found the fine arts section had beautiful books with paintings of birds. I also found an interesting book entitled, ***John James Audubon's Birds in Cross Stitch*** by Ginnie Thompson. This book includes color photographs of finished cross stitch birds as well as the patterns and directions. Each plate contains quotations taken from John James Audubon's five volume ***Ornithological Biography*** (1831-1839). It is interesting to compare the cross stitched color plates with the reproductions of Audubon's original paintings in the book listed above or in his great work, ***The Birds of America***. This is a good skills activity as well as a good observation activity because the children must use the index in Audubon's books to locate the desired reproductions. The third place I found books pertaining to birds in my library was in the Science and Technology Department. I could have literally come home with hundreds of books on birds! I realized that I had to put some boundaries on our study.

I want to encourage you to read the preface, introduction, or foreword to some of the books you choose. These sections supply informative details concerning Audubon's works and life. Years ago, I never read these parts of books because I felt it was a waste of time, but I now realize that valuable information can be gained from reading them. This is true for any book you read.

Library Books

The following books were located in the Fine Arts Department of my public library. ***Audubon, Homer, Whistler, and 19th Century America***, by John Wilmerding. (Although this only contains one color reproduction of Audubon's works, it contains biographical information about Audubon and beautiful color plates of other American artists who lived during the same time period.) ***Painting Birds***, by Susan Rayfield. ***Draw Birds***, by David Brown, a simple yet very informative paperback book that will enable your children to draw birds fairly easily. It even details the anatomy of various birds. *The Art of Robert Bateman*, by Ramsay Derry. Mr. Bateman is a modern naturalist. His book includes many paintings of birds. *John James Audubon's Birds in Cross Stitch*, by Ginnie Thompson. (Mentioned above.) *Bird*, an Eyewitness Book, published by Alfred A. Knopf. Contains great pictures. (Most of the books in the Eyewitness series are very well written. This series covers a vast range of titles from *Ancient Egypt* to *Tree*. Many libraries carry this series as well as many homeschool catalog companies.) *An Illustrated Guide to Attracting Birds*, Sunset Publishing Corporation. This focuses on bird identification, plant lists, feeders, houses, and baths. Use the subject card catalog in the Fine Arts Department to locate other books pertaining to birds.

The following books were located in the Science and Technology Department of my library. *The Miracle of Flight*, by Richard Cromer. This book explains the aerodynamics of flight and how a bird's physical structure enables it to fly. *The Birds of America*, by John James Audubon. (Mentioned above.) *Tunnicliffe's Birds, Measured Drawings*, by C.F. Tunnicliffe.

The following books were located in the Children's Department of my library. *How Birds Fly*, by Russell Freedman. (This book gives a simpler explanation than *The Miracle of Flight*.) *120 Questions and Answers About Birds*, by Madeline Angell. *State Birds*, By Arthur Singer and Alan Singer. Since there are so many kinds of birds that you can study, a simpler task would be to focus on our state birds. During this study the children can brush up on the location of each state. Arthur and Alan Singer worked together to paint the 1982 commemorative stamp block of birds and flowers for the fifty states for the U.S. Postal Service. If your children collect stamps, this may interest them. *Birds with Bracelets: The Story of Bird Banding*, by Susan F. Welty.

In the junior biography section I found several biographies about Audubon. I chose, Audubon, *The Man Who Painted Birds*, by Norah Smaridge. The last area where I found bird books was in the poetry section of the children's department. Browse through these books of poetry, using subject indexes to locate poems about birds. Some books I selected were: *Wings from the Wind*, An Anthology of Poems Selected and Illustrated by Tasha Tudor. *Sing a Song of Popcorn*, selected by B.S. deRegniers. *Feather or Fur*, by Grete Manheim. Using a poetry index in the reference section will help you to locate more poems about birds. You will also find many easy readers containing stories about birds. The subject card catalog will direct you to some of these books.

A related topic of study is of course the study of flight, predominantly the achievements man has made in aerodynamics. This can become very involved, and I think it best to give only an introduction into this now, and focus on the history of flight at a later time. *The Miracle of Flight* or *How Birds Fly* should be sufficient at this time for introducing the children to aerodynamics.

The ***Character Sketches Books***, published by Institute in Basic Life Principles, contain facinating information about various kinds of birds. These books are a superb reference for any nature study.

If you own a pet bird, that is great. Your children can observe the bird, making notes about behavior and making sketches. They can do this with birds in your neighborhood or a nearby park as well. A pair of binoculars would prove helpful for bird watching. Check out a simple library book on binoculars and find out how they work. Try to identify the birds in your neighborhood. How about buying or making a simple bird feeder to attract birds to your home? Is there a zoo with an aviary in your area? Take sketch pads to make drawings and record notes. Have the children compose a poem to go with their favorite sketch.

Your children can write to the National Audubon Society for information on their publications. The address is: 950 Third Avenue

New York, New York 10022

They may also write to the National Wildlife Federation: 1412 Sixteenth Street NW

Washington, DC 20036

Bible

Investigate Bible verses that mention birds. A topical Bible would prove helpful. Some suggested verses are: Genesis 1:20-30, the creation of birds on the fifth day and man's dominion over them along with the other creatures. Leviticus 11:13-20 concerning species that are unclean. Job 38:41, Psalm 147:9 concerning ravens. Matthew 10:29 and Luke 12:6, 24 concerning sparrows and ravens. Psalm 84:3, 124:7. Matthew 6:26, 8:20. Revelation 19:17. You will find many more and you may also look up "snare" in your concordance or topical Bible.

As is evident in all our studies, we are made aware of the complexity and beauty which our Heavenly Father created. Man can only make an inferior duplicate of the complicated wing of a bird. You will find that you could never complete a study of every kind of bird. And what scientist can explain bird migration apart from the plan of a Divine Creator?

Happy bird watching!

HUMAN BODY UNIT

Books and Materials

Backyard Scientist, Series Three, by Jane Hoffman. This book of experiments allows you to explore the life sciences. Some of the experiments included are: The Blinking Experiment, The Digestion Experiment, The Vocal Cord Experiment, The Nerve Cell Experiment, The Lung Experiment, The Ear Experiment, and more. The experiments found in Jane's books use items found around the home or items that are easily accessible. Another pleasing feature about the *Backyard Scientist* books is that each experiment includes a solution at the end. You are not left to figure things out for yourself if you are having trouble. *The Gray's Anatomy Coloring Book*, published by Running Press. This book includes over a hundred adaptations of the original illustrations from the classic reference book, *Gray's Anatomy*. It includes descriptive captions, and the terminology has been limited to the basics so as not to be overwhelming. *The Human Body*, by Jonathan Miller. This fun book contains three-dimensional, movable illustrations showing the workings of the human body. Another valuable resource is the *Pocket Science Kit, Human Senses and Body Parts*. This pocket kit includes a folder with 48 reproducible activity sheets pertaining to the human body. *Somebody*, the human anatomy game by Aristoplay, is a game/puzzle activity that helps teach the names, locations, and functions of the body parts.

Library Books

Your Body and How It Works, by Ovid K. Wong, Ph.D. I used this book for dictation exercises and for conducting interesting experiments. The chapters included are: The Covering System, The Supportive System, The Muscular System, the Circulatory System, the Breathing System, The Digestive System, The Waste-Disposal System, The Hormonal System, The Nervous System, and the Reproductive System. The book also includes a glossary of terms. Each section contains pertinent experiments which also include conclusions. (The conclusions are to help us moms!) I really enjoy this book as it is clear, concise, and uncomplicated. It even provides older children with a good functional study of the body. (Ignore the introduction about the body being a complicated machine, or use it to discuss this humanistic falsehood.) *Your Body is Wonderfully Made*, by Fred B. Rogers, M.D. A simple yet refreshing little book that emphasizes the Biblical reference in Psalms that man is "wonderfully made." It states that the body functions more smoothly and intricately than any engineering marvel ever envisioned. (A sharp contrast to the "we are machines" concept.) This book can be read in one sitting and is a good choice for your children to read aloud. ***The Human Body, Your Body and How it Works***, by Ruth Dowling Bruun, M.D. and Berttel Bruun, M.D. Offering a more in depth look at the body with excellent colored drawings. ***How & Why, A Kid's Book About the Body***, by Catherine O'Neil. Addresses questions such as: How does my brain tell my legs to move when I go for a walk? What would happen if I didn't have thumbs? Why do I have a belly button? How do I see? Why does it hurt to get a burn or cut? ***The Skeleton Inside You***, by Philip Balestrino. A simple book that young children can read aloud. ***Leonardo Da Vinci, Art for Children***, by Ernest Raboff. This is a simple book about Da Vinci, however, you can locate other books in the fine arts section of your library that contain quality reproductions of his work. Among other things, Da Vinci was an artist who studied portraiture which involved the study of anatomy. It is interesting to observe the accuracy with which he painted the human form.

The following books are about individuals who worked to improve the quality of life for man. These biographies offer a bit of historical emphasis to your study. ***Dr. William Harvey and the Discovery of Circulation***, by William C. Harrison. The answers that Harvey found about the circulation of the blood didn't agree with the beliefs and practices of his time. (He was born in 1578.) He knew it was dangerous to express ideas that opposed those then in acceptance. Even the brilliant Galileo had been persecuted for expressing new truths about the universe. ***Dr. Beaumont and the Man with the Hole in His Stomach***, by Sam and Beryl Epstein. As a result of a shooting accident, a frontiersman was left with a hole in his stomach that would never close up. Doctor Beaumont performed experiments on digestion through this passageway. ***The Mysterious Rays, Marie Curie's World***, by Nancy Veglahn. Marie Curie discovered radium. During the First World War she equipped a mobile x-ray unit and accompanied it to hospitals on the battle field. The unit was used to locate broken bones and shell fragments. ***Famous Firsts in Medicine***, by Bette Crook and Charles L. Crook, M.D. ***Patriot Doctor, the Story of Benjamin Rush***, by Esther M. Douty. Benjamin Rush was a doctor, teacher, patriot, and humanitarian. As physician-general of Washington's armies, he fought death and disease through the desperate years of the Revolution. Rush collaborated with Thomas Paine on ***Common Sense***, and as a congressman was a signer of the Declaration of Independence.

Bible

This unit provides us with an opportunity to study the most magnificent handiwork of the Creator. Naturally the first place we turn to is the book of Genesis.
Genesis 1:26-27.

> *And God said, 'Let us make man in our image, after our likeness; and let them have dominion over the fish of the sea, and over the fowl of the air, and over the cattle, and over all the earth, and over every creeping thing that creepeth upon the earth.' So God created man in his own image, in the image of God created he him; male and female created he them.*

Genesis 2:7.

> *And the Lord God formed man of the dust of the ground, and breathed into his nostrils the breath of life; and man became a living soul.*

Some other verses are Job 10:8-12, Job 33:4, Job 43:19, Psalm 119:73, Psalm 138:8, Psalm 139:13-16, Isaiah 64:8, Job 32:8, Matthew 6:22-23.

Using a concordance, look up words relating to the body such as body, bone, blood, breath, circumcise, ears, face, feet, finger, flesh, forehead, hand, heal, heart, illness, infection, infirmities, knee, life, mouth, multiply, neck, physician, sick, skin, skull, soul, taste, tears, teeth, temple, thirst, throat, tongue, tooth, vessel, voice, weep, and womb.

My favorite passage for this human body unit is Psalm 139:13-16. My children and I memorized this passage. I prefer the New American Standard Version that reads:

> *For Thou didst form my inward parts;*
> *Thou didst weave me in my mother's womb.*
> *I will give thanks to Thee, for I am fearfully and wonderfully made;*
> *Wonderful are Thy works,*
> *And my soul knows it very well.*
> *My frame was not hidden from Thee,*
> *When I was made in secret,*
> *And skillfully wrought in the depths of the earth.*
> *Thine eyes have seen my unformed substance;*
> *And in Thy book they were all written,*
> *The days that were ordained for me,*
> *When as yet there was not one of them.*

This passage and others make excellent typing exercises. We use a large print Bible for typing practice. Another interesting Biblical passage to study in the course of this unit is Ephesians 6:13-17.

Therefore, take up the full armor of God, that you may be able to resist the evil day, and having done everything, to stand firm. Stand firm therefore, having girded your loins with truth, and having put on the breastplate of righteousness, and having shod your feet with the preparation of the gospel of peace; in addition to all, take up the shield of faith with which you will be able to extinguish all the flaming missiles of the evil one. And take the helmet of salvation, and the sword of the Spirit, which is the word of God.

Have your children note the various body parts mentioned and what protects them.

Language Arts and Science

The book *Your Body and How It Works*, by Wong, makes an excellent choice for selecting passages for your children to either copy or take by dictation. Each chapter covers a different system and has a number of experiments relating to that system. Read the chapter with your children, allowing capable children to read portions aloud, then select the most pertinent information to be copied or dictated. For young children this may mean only a sentence or two or key words relative to that system. Older children may copy the entire chapter, usually two or three pages. As you explore each body system, have your children color corresponding illustrations from the *Gray's Anatomy Coloring Book*. Then choose one or two of the experiments to perform. Jane Hoffman's *Backyard Science Series Three* also has clever experiments for understanding the body systems. I encourage you to have your children copy the experimental procedures outlined in the books and then to record their findings. This provides them with a good model for recording experimental procedures. Perhaps you and your children can devise an experiment of your own during this unit. Write out the materials, procedures and conclusions as modeled in the books.

While undergoing the experiments, have your children make accompanying illustrations to help fix the new found information in their minds. This can be as simple as tracing a picture from the *Gray's Anatomy Coloring Book* that corresponds to the system you are investigating.

After studying each system, have your children make a list of all the words they can think of that relate to that particular system. Children who are more artistic can write the words in such a manner as to form a picture of something indicative of that body system.

Take some large butcher paper, parcel packaging paper, or lots of plain newsprint taped together. Have your child lay on it, and trace his basic body shape. Then let him add hair, nails, skin color, eyes, nose, mouth, ears, teeth, heart, lungs, blood vessels, and all the other organs. He will probably need to use a book or the game *Somebody* to help him out. He can even tape overlays on his body that flip up to reveal other body parts underneath. These "bodies" can be rolled up for easy storage.

Poetry is always fun to explore. Psalm 139:13-16 is a beautiful poem about the marvelous formation of an infant in the womb. The children can take the word lists they compiled for each system and make a poem about one or all the systems combined. You may need to help them think of adjectives and verbs relating to each system as most of the words on their lists may be nouns. Remind them that poems do not have to rhyme. The feeling evoked by the poem is more important.

You will find many library books about the human body. Choose some books you like to read aloud with your children or have them read on their own. The book I chose to use as our basic text was rather simple. I wanted to give my children an overview of the workings of the body. Later we will study each individual system in greater depth. Taking two systems, it will take five units to make this more in depth study. Other units will be interspersed between them. Don't think you must cover everything in just one unit. Remember, learning lasts a lifetime. The body is our Maker's most magnificent creation, so it is fitting that we should come back to it time after time. It helps us to recall that we are fearfully and wonderfully made, and we are precious in His sight!

ELECTRICITY UNIT

Library Books

Giants of Electricity, by Percy Dunsheath. This book includes biographical information about numerous scientists who contributed to the harnessing of electricity: Ampre, Davy, Faraday, Franklin, Galvani, Gauss, Henry, Kelvin, Maxwell, Oersted, Olim, Volta, and Weber. *The Quest of Michael Faraday*, by Tad Harvey. Faraday discovered how to produce electricity from magnetism. *Charles Proteus Steinmetz, Wizard of Electricity*, by Erick Berry. This is the story of a crippled mathematical genius with a humped back and large head. *How Did We Find Out About Electricity?*, by Isaac Asimov. Asimov tells the history of electricity from the early Greek philosophers to Volta's battery and Faraday's electromagnetism. *The Thomas Edison Book of Easy and Incredible Experiments*, by James G. Cook and the Thomas Alva Edison Foundation. Experiments in this book encompass magnetism, electricity, electrochemistry, chemistry, physics, energy, and environmental studies. *The Way Things Work*, by David Macaulay. Yes, I'm recommending this book again. Macaulay is both entertaining and instructive in his comprehensive book that explains the mysteries behind the things we encounter everyday. Specifically pertaining to this unit are the sections on electricity in general, magnetism, electromagnetism, the electric bell, the electric horn, the electric motor, the electric generator, the two-way switch, batteries, circuits, current, and more. Macaulay's reference book should be included in the homeschooling family's home. *Electricity and Magnets*, by Barbara Taylor. This is a nice simple book. The table of contents reads: Using Electricity, Sparks and Flashes, Batteries, Circuits, Magnetic Forces, and Electromagnetics. The book also includes step-by-step investigations.

The next two books are extremely simple. *Experiments with Electricity and Experiments with Magnets*, both by Helen Challand. *Switch On, Switch Off*, by Melvin Berger. This provides a young child with an easy introduction to electricity. *Discovering Electricity*, by Rae Bains. This is another good introductory book. *Bright Lights to See By*, by Miriam Anne Bourne. A delightful story about a period in history when electricity was still a wonder.

You will find several biographies of the famous scientists who contributed to the harnessing of electricity. If you have trouble locating some of the suggested books, look for biographies of the men mentioned. You will also find many books relating to electricity in the children's section of your library. Use your subject card catalog to locate them.

When undertaking scientific units, I am more successful if I stick with simple books that present basic facts. Later, these scientific topics can be studied in greater depth, but a good foundation must first be laid. Tedious facts are often difficult to memorize, but basic concepts that are presented in a simple and concise fashion enable us to progress to more difficult concepts. Therefore, we build upon previous knowledge rather than memorize more and more nebulous facts.

An exciting aspect of science is that the so called "laws of nature" are fixed and unchanging. This is because an omnipotent and immutable Creator designed our universe. If the universe just happened, how could we rely on these laws of nature to remain constant?

Quoting from *Scientific Creationism*, by Henry Morris:

It seems obvious that the evolution model would predict that matter, energy and the laws are still evolving since they must have evolved in the past and there is no external agent to bring such evolution to a halt.

*Creationists obviously would predict that the basic laws as well as the fundamental nature of matter and energy, would not now be changing at all. They were completely created - **finished** in the past, and are being **conserved** in the present.*

Michael Faraday was an English scientist who we credit more than any other single man with giving us the Age of Electricity. He felt that all of nature was governed by a few fixed and unchanging laws. He was a great and thorough experimenter. He set up experiments to test his theories, realizing that if an experiment failed to prove his theory, the flaw was with himself, not with nature. Either his experiment or his theory was imperfect.

As you study electricity, or any science-based unit, it is fitting to also study the immutability of the Creator. Just as the laws of nature are unchanging, so are His ways, His thoughts, and His laws unchanging. He is the same yesterday, today, and tomorrow. Some verses (KJV) to reflect on are: Ecclesiastes 3:14, *"Whatsoever God doeth, it shall be for ever; nothing can be put to it, nor anything taken from it."* Malachi 3:6 *"I am the LORD, I change not; therefore ye sons of Jacob are not consumed."* James 1:17 *"Every good gift and every perfect gift is from above, and cometh down from the Father of lights, with whom is no variableness, neither shadow of turning."* Use a topical Bible and look up "GOD-Immutable" to find other pertinent verses. A very interesting and informative little book dealing with the attributes of the Almighty is entitled, *The Knowledge of the Holy*, by A.W. Tozer.

As with most other science units, this unit on electricity lends itself well to projects or experiments. Using some simple library books you can conduct a few experiments with your children. I like the way the experiments are laid out in *The Thomas Edison Book of Easy and Incredible Experiments*. (There are several library books available that offer simple experiments with electricity.) Part I of the Thomas Edison book is entitled, Simple Experiments in Electricity, Electrochemistry, and Basic Chemistry. Some of the experiments in this section are A Simple Electrical Circuit, How a Doorbell Circuit Works, How a Two-Way Switch Works, Conductors and Insulators, What is an Electrolyte?, Electricity from a Lemon, The First Electric Battery. Part II, Simple Experiments in Magnetism and Electricity, include some of the following experiments: The Variable Conductivity of Carbon, The Carbon Transmitter Principle, Making an Electromagnet, Magnetism and the Compass, the Fuse in Action, Faraday's "Ice-pail" Experiment, and Does Ice Conduct Electricity? This book offers many more experiments using inexpensive, easy-to-obtain materials. Another interesting feature of the book is that it contains photos of Thomas Alva Edison himself as well as a chronology of events in his life.

While conducting experiments with electricity, it is helpful for the children to keep a log of the materials used, procedures carried out, and the results noted. It is also beneficial to record the reasoning behind their findings. Making illustrations of the procedures will also aid your child's retention of his findings.

A fun and inexpensive game you may want to purchase is *AC/DC Electric Circuit Game* manufactured by Ampersand Press. (See resource guide for ordering information.) This game is played with a special deck of cards. The cards illustrate wires, switches, energy sources, energy users, and fuses. The object of the game is to build workable circuits. The players may get "shocked" or "shorted." This game offers an intriguing introduction to the study of electricity.

Use a simple library book about electricity and have your children write each word found in the glossary on one side of an index card. Then have them write the meaning of the word on the reverse side of the card. These cards can be used to quiz the children on their vocabulary. Another alternative is to write a word on one card and the meaning of that word on a separate card. Then the cards can be mixed and then matched.

Younger children can be sent on a hunt to find items in the house that operate on electricity. Older children can work some calculations using past electric bills. How much electricity do you use on the average per day in a given month? How much more or how much less electricity did you use this month than you used last month? How many kilowatt hours did you purchase this month? What is a kilowatt hour? How much do you pay per kilowatt hour? Discuss the other points of your electric bill. (Usually all the terminology and method of calculation are defined on the back of your bill.) Have your children make a list of things they can do to help conserve energy and thus lower your electric bill

Remember, when you are conducting a unit requiring a lot of experiments or projects, lighten up on the more academic aspects of the unit. These projects "teach" so many principles and disciplines that you do not need to "pad" them with an abundance of written work. Keeping a record of the experiment should suffice in such units. Also read topic-related books with your children and have fun!

HISTORY AND GEOGRAPHY

FOREIGN COUNTRIES UNIT

We open up new horizons for ourselves and our children as we examine the geography and culture of other lands. It can be difficult for our children to see beyond our neighborhood, let alone across the world. A useful book to read with younger children is, *Where in the World do You Live*, by Al Hine and John Alcorn.

When we begin a study of another country, it is helpful to first examine the term "country." According to National Geographic Society's *Exploring Our World, The Adventure of Geography*, "A country is a recognized territory whose government is the highest legal authority over the land and the people living within its boundaries. Each country has not only distinct boundaries, but also a unique name and flag. All but the smallest countries issue their own money."

Do you know how many countries there are in the world? Experts disagree on the number because they disagree about the status of some territories. An important measuring device is whether the governments of other countries recognize a region as independent and self-governing.

The term "state" is often used to mean "country," although it is a more formal term. "Nation" is also frequently used in place of "country." "Nation" denotes a group of people with a common culture who may be divided by political boundaries.

Spend some time with your children perusing a map of the world or a globe. Have the capable children read the names of a number of countries. Choose one continent and learn the names of all its countries. Aristoplay has a terrific game called *Where in The World?*, an excellent device for learning the names and locations of countries. Many other pertinent facts can be learned as well. Select a country from the continent you have chosen and begin a study of it. Learn the names of important bodies of water, mountains, and other geographical features located in and around the country you have chosen. *Exploring Your World, The Adventure of Geography* is an excellent resource that enables readers to explore the "how's" and "why's" of our planet as well as the "where's." Its concise text and vivid photographs acquaint us with terms such as canal, continent, desert, earthquake, grassland, island, mountain, plateau, and more. A very simple library book that is useful for young children is *Geography from A to Z, A Picture Glossary*, by Jack Knowlton. Another is *The Viking Children's World Atlas: An Introductory Atlas for Young People*.

Select library books pertaining to your country of interest, remembering to investigate clothing, art, sports, literature, music, cuisine, theatre, education, government, hobbies, economy, religion, language, alphabet, geography, and as many other areas as you can imagine. How does this country relate to the countries surrounding it, and what influences have these neighboring countries had on one another's pasts? Skim your local newspaper for information on political happenings today. *God's World Newspaper* offers interesting and well written newspapers for children beginning at the kindergarten level and extending through the high school level. They even offer papers for adults.

Video tapes offer us a bird's eye view of the country we are investigating. Public libraries or video rental stores are an excellent source for video cassette tapes pertaining to foreign countries. Your library will probably own audio cassette tapes featuring a study of the language(s) of your chosen country of study. Investigate the children's section for language tapes which present the language in a simple format. You and your children may want to learn a few phrases in the foreign tongue.

Audio Memory Publishing offers two audio cassette tapes that make learning the names of the countries a simple task. The states of the U.S., territories of Canada, and the planets of the Solar System are included as well. The tapes are simply titled, *Geography Songs* and *More Geography Songs*.

When conducting an historical unit, or most any other unit, it is advantageous to make a time-line and time-line figures to represent the historical figures of study.

For further information concerning time-lines, see my book *How to Create Your Own Unit Study*, pages 25-26. Watch for a future publication entitled, *The Timeline Portfolio*.

KOREA

Korea lies in close proximity to both China and Japan. Only a short stretch of water separates the Korean and Japanese coasts. Both the Chinese and Japanese have exerted an influence over Korea in the course of history. At various times armies of both China and Japan have invaded Korea and imposed their social and political institutions on it. Korea has therefore adopted some of the culture of these nations. However, the independent nature of Korea has enabled it to retain its own distinct civilization for thousands of years. In the 1800's Korea was known as the hermit kingdom.

Library Books

Korea: Land of the Morning Calm, by Carol Farley. A very informative book that offers a brief but well written account of modern Korea and its past. This book will direct you to many areas of interest to be pursued. I suggest this as a basic text for your study. Its information is current as it was published in 1991. Many older library books suffice for a study of Korea's past, but do not give appropriate information concerning Korea today. *Koreans*, by Jodine Mayberry. Another recent and interesting publication offering a brief treatment of Korea and a look at the Koreans who have immigrated to America. *Korea*, by Karen Jacobsen. A simple book for the primary level. A good choice as a read aloud book for beginning readers. *We Don't Look Like Our Mom and Dad*, by Harriet Langsam Sobol. A photo-essay on the life of an American family and their two Korean-born adopted sons. *My Best Friend Mee-Yung Kim*, by Dianne MacMillan and Dorothy Freeman. *We Adopted You, Benjamin Koo*, by Linda Walvoord Girard. *Ms. Isabelle Cornell, Herself*, by Carol Farley. I suggest only using the information in the back of this book concerning the Korean alphabet, Hangul. The book itself depicts a young American girl who unwillingly moves with her mom and step-father to Korea for two years. The girl is rude and disrespectful to her parents. However, the information in the back of the book concerning Hangul is extremely helpful. *Counting Your Way Through Korea*, by Jim Haskins. Korean life is explored as you learn to count from one through ten in Korean. Haskins describes such aspects as **one** ancient building and **four** parts of the traditional Korean costume for men. *Courage in Korea: Stories of the Korean War*, selected by Albert Tibbets. This volume contains ten stories of the U.N. resistance to the Red invasion of Korea. It's about men in foxholes, in rice paddies, in waist-deep mud, making a firm stand against the intruders. The courage and friendship of these men are evident as you are exposed to the hardships and suffering they endured as they said to the Communists, "No Farther." I stayed up late at night reading this book because it was so interesting. If you begin one story, you must finish it without delay. Most of the stories selected for publication in *Courage in Korea* were written in the early 1950's. ***Bong Nam and the Pheasants***, story retold by Edward Yushin Yoo. A delightful Korean tale. ***Aekyung's Dream***, by Min Paek. A story of a young Korean girl who immigrated to America with her family; a contemporary tale from the North American Korean Community. The author has also translated the text into Korean. ***The Cat Who Went To Heaven***, by Elizabeth Coatsworth. This Newbery Award book relates the tale concerning a poor Japanese artist who was commissioned to paint the death of the lord Buddha. It is a fine literary work which will acquaint your children with the religious beliefs prevalent in much of the Far East, including Korea. ***Cooking the Korean Way***, by Okwha Chung and Judy Monore. Besides offering simple Korean dishes you can make at home, the book gives a brief introduction to the land, history, food, and feasts of Korea. ***Understanding Far Eastern Art***, by Julia Hutt. A complete guide to the art of China, Japan, and Korea, detailing ceramics, sculpture, painting, prints, lacquer, textiles, and metalwork. ***The Oriental World***, by Jeannine Auboyer and Roger Goepper. 228 illustrations of art from India, South-East Asia, China, Korea, and Japan. ***Chinese and Oriental Art***, by Michael Batterberry. Includes a very informative section on Korean art. Batterberry does an excellent job of weaving history and art into an interesting text. ***Kiteworks: Explorations in Kite Building and Flying***, by Maxwell Eden. ***Catch the Wind!: All About Kites***, by Gail Gibbons. A simple book telling about the basic materials for kites, how kites are made, who were the first kite flyers, and how kites take off and fly. Includes step-by-step instructions for building a kite. Bright and colorful; great for young children. ***Tae Kwon Do: The Korean Martial Art***, by Richard Chun. Tae Kwon Do literally means "The Art of Kicking and Punching." This book contains an interesting history of the Korean martial art. Another similar book is ***Tae Kwon Do: The Ultimate Reference Guide to the World's Most Popular Martial Art***, by Yeon Hee Park, Yeon Hwan Park, and Jon Gerrard. ***Vocabulearn Korean***, consists of two 90-minute audio cassettes and a 36 page Vocabulist. Another cassette tape program I found at my public library is entitled ***Language/30 - Korean***. This program consists of two audio cassettes and a phrase dictionary. Everyday words and phrases are emphasized. Your library may contain other instructional language cassettes. These are interesting to listen to, and they give you and your children an opportunity to experience the language. Your public library may also own videos on Korea. Video rental stores carry a variety of travel videos including presentations of Korea.

Other Books and Materials

Exploring Your World, the Adventure of Geography, published by the National Geographic Society. This book is a valuable resource which will assist you as you encounter geographical terms. For example, when studying Korea you encounter inactive volcanoes, mountains, seas, rivers, peninsulas, islands, monsoons, the Pacific Ocean, and so on. *Exploring Your World* offers superb pictures and text depicting geographical terms. *Operation World*, by Patrick Johnstone. A day-to-day guide to praying for the world. *Operation World* is a prayer calendar covering every country in the world. Background facts and figures include populations, peoples, economies, politics, religions and churches. Accompanying the book are prayer cards for spiritually needy nations. Each card represents one country and includes facts as well as a list of the basic prayer needs of that particular country. It is very exciting to read about the impact the Christian church has had in South Korea. Christianity as well as other religions have been harshly repressed in North Korea.

Korean Embassies and Consulates in the U.S.

Embassy of Korea
2370 Massachusetts Avenue, N.W.
Washington, DC 20008
(202) 939-5600

Korean Consulate General
3500 Clay Street
San Francisco, CA 94118
(415) 921-2251

There are many officials and their families living in the U.S. who are affiliated with the Korean Embassy. They would probably like to receive letters from children requesting information concerning their country. Your children may even find an intriguing pen pal amongst the children of the Korean Embassy officials.

Religion

The major religions of Korea are Buddhism, Confucianism, and Christianity.

Koreans celebrate Buddha's birthday as the Feast of Lanterns. Lanterns are displayed in the temple courtyards as symbolic of the light Buddha brought to the world. Buddhism came to Korea as an influence of the people of India. Perhaps your children would like to construct a paper lantern fashioned after the Korean lanterns.

Confucianism was implemented in Korea through the influence of the Chinese. Confucius believed that a strict social order would benefit society. The Confucian teaching of social order still controls Korean life today. Confucius also sought to help people live a good life in the present, rather than planning for a future in heaven.

Christianity reached South Korea in the nineteenth century. The Christian church with the largest membership in the world today is located in Yoido. It has a membership of over 629,000. North Korea is said to have 10,000 Christians in Pyongyang.

Other Areas of Interest

Koreans are noted for their magnificent pottery called celadon, a pottery with a greenish blue glaze. Using books from the library, investigate this art form and read about its history. In the index of these library books, you can look up Korea, and find many interesting pictures and descriptions of beautiful Korean art. The Koreans have a fondness for dragons as is evident from their ancient architecture. Kites offer another avenue to explore as the Koreans enjoy kite flying contests. A library book about kites will enable you to make kites and have a contest of your own. Investigate the Korean alphabet, Hangul. Hangul is a writing system that consists of 24 symbols based on sounds, rather than thousands of Chinese characters based on meanings. This system was developed during the reign of King Sejong, ruler of Korea from 1418 to 1450. He decided that a simpler writing system should be devised so that all people could learn to read and write. At certain times during Korea's history, Hangul was forbidden. Today it is very highly regarded and the Korean people celebrate National Hangul Day. The people of South Korea enjoy a very high literacy rate as a result of the implementation of this writing system. Using the information in the back of the book, *Ms. Isabelle Cornell, Herself*, your children can write messages to each other in Hangul. The book, *Aekyung's Dream* is written in English as well as Hangul.

Have your children try their hand at translating a few lines from Hangul into English. Cover the English portion and no peeking! Note the formation of the symbols used in Hangul. Locate some examples of Chinese and Japanese writing and compare them with the symbols of Hangul. Discuss how the use of a writing system based on sounds is more efficient than one based on characters representing separate ideas. During the same century Hangul was developed, the Koreans were printing with movable type. This remarkable feat began in 1403, some 50 years before Johann Gutenberg invented his printing press. Prepare a Korean meal or dish, decorating the table in Korean fashion for an added touch. *Cooking the Korean Way* offers a variety of recipes, including the Korean national dish, Kimch'i. It is made of pickled cabbage and ranges from mild to very spicy.

Traditional Korean dress is another area of interest. *Understanding Far Eastern Art* includes some information on the textiles of the far east, and concentrates on the design of the kimono. Costume books offer additional material concerning the traditional dress. The Amazon Dry Goods Company has authentic patterns for various far eastern dress for more industrious families. (See resource guide for ordering information.) Perhaps your family would like to learn the Korean national anthem, "Aegugka." As you study the history of Korea, you can discuss the differences between North and South Korea with your children. For example, in North Korea, state education is implemented at three months of age when babies must attend state-owned nurseries. Contrast this with South Korea where family life plays a vital role. A study of Tae Kwon Do, an ancient art of self defense will undoubtedly prove inviting to many children. Investigate other traditional and popular Korean sports.

Geography

Explore the vast mountain ranges of Korea. Investigate its extinct volcanoes, its fierce monsoons, its seas and rivers, its three thousand islands, and its green rice fields. Define these terms with your children. Also define the term peninsula which describes Korea as a whole. Video cassettes will probably offer the best views of Korea's geography. Unfortunately, I have not found many library books with numerous quality photographs of Korea. If you have an opportunity you might peruse some of the National Geographic Magazines. Investigate magazines and newspapers which will shed light on the political activity in Korea today. This can be done by skimming your local newspaper, or using the facilities provided at your public library.

Activity

As your children study various countries of the world, have them compile an atlas. This can include copy or dictation work about the areas of interest pertaining to each country; maps the children have collected, traced, or drawn; facts about the people, land, government, and so on; pictures depicting the dress of the country; poems they have written or copied about the country; photographs of any projects they have made relative to their study; and other useful materials. These atlases can be kept for future reference and serve as a tool for review.

ANCIENT EGYPT

Library Books

The Art of Egypt Under the Pharaohs, by Shirley Glubok. This text examines artistic Egyptian achievements through a discussion of the history, mythology, daily life, customs, and religious beliefs of the ancient Egyptians. *The Art of Ancient Egypt*, by Shirley Glubok. An excellent introduction to the art of ancient Egypt related in an uncomplicated style. *Looking at Architecture*, by Roberta M. Paine. A book spanning the centuries from ancient Egypt to the present day that describes the intellect and human effort involved in the designing and erection of many famous buildings. *The Buildings of Ancient Egypt*, written and illustrated by Helen and Richard Leacroft. Archaeologists have been able to re-create an image of life in Ancient Egypt more than three thousand years ago as a result of exploring tombs and their contents. *Ancient Egypt, An Eyewitness Book*, by George Hart. Real-life photographs and an informative text present us with a mini-museum through which we can view early Egyptian life. *Science in Ancient Egypt*, by Geraldine Woods. Chapter contents include: Geography and Ancient Egyptian Science, The Pyramids, Mathematics, Astronomy and Timekeeping, Medicine, Writing and Agriculture, Crafts and Technology, and Our Debt to Egypt. *Pyramid*, by David Macaulay. Pyramids stand today as massive remnants of ancient Egyptian culture. Mr. Macaulay takes us through the step-by-step construction of an imaginary pyramid. *Ancient Egypt*, by Daniel Cohen. Each page is almost filled with beautiful color drawings depicting life in early Egypt. *The Way Things Work*, by David Macaulay contains simple yet sufficient information about levers, pulleys, inclined planes, and related topics. This works well in conjunction with Macaulay's book, *Pyramid*, which incorporates a discussion of such mechanical devices. (Although this book is available in most public libraries, it is a valuable reference tool to own.) *Exodus: Adapted From the Bible*, by Miriam Chaikin, illustrated by Charles Mikolaycak. The beautiful illustrations are a result of careful research into the ancient Egyptian world.

Other Books and Materials

Pocket Science: Simple Tools and Machines. An easy-to-use kit that allows you to make gears that really work, two types of pulleys, an inclined plane, and more. While learning about simple tools you are building a foundation for understanding more complex devices. Work sheets and a tool mobile are included.

A great hands on accompaniment for Macaulay's *Pyramid* and *The Way Things Work*. *Pyramids and Mummies: A Puzzling Game of Discovery and Intrigue*, by Aristoplay. Build a pyramid as you decipher messages in cryptic rebus writing.

I am delighted to have found an excellent resource for obtaining materials for historically based units. Rob and Cyndy Shearer of Greenleaf Press have written study guides for various time periods including *The Greenleaf Guide to Ancient Egypt, The Greenleaf Guide to Famous Men of Greece, The Greenleaf Guide to Famous Men of Rome*, and T*he Greenleaf Guide to Famous Men of the Middle Ages*. They have written these guides to accompany *Pharaohs of Ancient Egypt* (Landmark Books), *Famous Men of Greece, Famous Men of Rome*, and *Famous Men of the Middle Ages*. (The latter three were originally written by Haaren and have been edited and updated by Rob and Cyndy.) The Greenleaf Catalog includes additional materials for a study of these areas mentioned as well as materials for a study of Vikings, Renaissance and Reformation, Explorers, and U.S. History. Their catalog is a terrific resource for historically based units as some books included are available from the public library. Greenleaf offers very good prices on their study packages which include the *Famous Men of ...* books, additional high quality publications relative to the study, and the *Greenleaf Guides*. The guides include suggestions for how to set your study of ancient civilizations in a Biblical context. They also offer suggestions for utilizing the additional books included in the package. All the books may be bought separately.

Greenleaf's Ancient Egypt Study Package includes: *Greenleaf Guide to Ancient Egypt*, by Cyndy Shearer; *The Pharaohs of Ancient Egypt*, by Elizabeth Payne; *Usborne Time Traveller Book of Pharaohs and Pyramids*, by Tony Allan; *Usborne First Travellers: Deserts*, by Angela Wilkes; *Pyramid*, by David Macaulay; *Tut's Mummy Lost...and Found*, by Judy Donnelly; and *Mummies Made in Egypt*, by Aliki. Greenleaf also offers other pertinent books for a study of Ancient Egypt including: *Cultural Atlas of Ancient Egypt; Young Scientist Book of Archaeology*, by Usborne; *Mara, Daughter of the Nile*, by Eloise Jarvis McGraw; *The Golden Goblet*, by Eloise Jarvis McGraw; *Pyramid - The Video*, based on David Macaulay's book, *Pyramid*.

You may be able to locate a good number of these books in your public library as well as some I listed at the beginning of this unit. The Greenleaf guides are so well written that I strongly urge you to purchase them. I'd like to give you a glimpse into these guides.

The Greenleaf Guides are primarily written for the elementary grades, but the information covered is so well laid out and interesting that older students would definitely benefit from their use. When I was in high school, history was a blur of dates and wars. Because I had an ability to memorize material fairly quickly, I managed to make good grades. The understanding behind all those facts was missing. Had I first been introduced to stories about the people of various times and cultures, I would have had some background knowledge upon which to hang the new information presented to me. Knowledge builds upon knowledge.

Greenleaf holds to this same philosophy. Quoting from their guides:

> *"Textbooks, by themselves, teach you facts. They do not introduce you to real people. Teaching history to elementary school students should be like calling a child to storytime. You find a snug comfortable place, you curl up together, and you start with `Once upon a time....'"*

Before beginning a study of Ancient Egypt, Greenleaf suggests that you put the study in Biblical context by reviewing the first few chapters of Genesis and noting the descriptions of those who followed Adam and his sons. They also suggest reading and discussing the story of the Tower of Babel. After this material is covered they urge you to move on to the first chapter of Romans to investigate what happens when man turns away from the truth and exchanges it for a lie. Next a review of Exodus is recommended. *The Greenleaf Guide* gives suggestions for covering this material.

The Greenleaf Guide gently takes you through the study, making recommendations along the way, but taking into account that each individual family will tackle the unit in a different manner. Suggested vocabulary lists from the recommended books are given, and various projects are listed such as making a salt map of Egypt. Other interesting pertinent tidbits are included such as a cryptogram, directions for the Egyptian game Senet and more. Other interest areas covered include a study of pyramids, levers, wheels, pulleys, inclined planes, basket weaving, the history of paper, deserts, irrigation, Egyptian boats, Pharaohs, the Nile River, archaeology, hieroglyphics, and more.

If you are interested in involving your family in a fascinating Bible study, this should be your beginning unit.

ANCIENT GREECE

Library Books

Ancient Greece, by Daniel Cohen. Colorful drawings adorn the easy-to-read text for an appealing treatment of early Greece. The book briefly covers the Trojan War, the Iliad, The Odyssey, Homer, Mycenae, The Bull of Minos, Plato, Atlantis, The Olympics, Military Life, Rule by the People, The Persain Wars, Gods and Goddesses, Tragedy and Comedy, Philosophers, and more. *The Everyday Life of a Greek Potter*, by Giovanni Caselli. *The Buildings of Ancient Greece*, by Helen and Richard Leacroft. These book takes us from the first simple huts of early Greece to the Classical period of Greece resulting in the superb buildings of Athens. *Art Tells a Story: Greek and Roman Myths*, by Penelope Proddow. The author tells the story of the myth behind each selected work of art after which she describes the work from the artistic point of view. *The Odyssey*, retold by Robin Lister and illustrated by Alan Baker. A colorful rendition of the ancient tale of Odysseus's journey from Troy. *The Children's Homer: The Adventures of Odysseus and the Tale of Troy*, by Padraic Colum. Mr. Colum proves himself a master storyteller in his retelling of these epic adventures. (See further discussion of this book later.)

Books and Other Materials

Greek Myths and Legends, by Aristoplay. A card game that enables your family to learn about mythology as you play "fish" with beautifully illustrated stories. *By Jove, By Jove Stories: Classical Adventure*, by Aristoplay. A fast-paced board game that offers an interesting introduction to classical myths. A 64 page book, by *Jove Stories* is included. The book also contains a pronunciation guide and index. *A First Dictionary of Cultural Literacy*, by E.D. Hirsch, Jr. Among many other useful topics, this book contains helpful information about mythology. A handy reference tool that includes sufficient information that is neither too technical nor too lengthy.

Much of the culture of many ancient civilizations is still intact today. If you were to visit Egypt, Greece, or Rome, you would find that monuments and ruins exist as reminders of the past.

Most of us have not been able to travel to these foreign lands, but we can learn from those who have. This can be accomplished by means of published materials such as books, maps, and videos, or on a more personal level by inquiring of friends or relatives who have traveled extensively. They may have returned from their excursions with articles, photographs, slides, or movies. Ask family members, friends, or church members if they have traveled to other countries. You may be pleasantly surprised to find someone who is more than willing to share their acquired knowledge with you. Investigate sources such as your public library or video rental store for movies of Ancient Greece.

Once again Greenleaf Press gets my vote for publishing excellent materials for historically based unit studies. (For further information about Greenleaf Press, refer to the *Ancient Egypt Unit Study*.) Rob and Cyndy Shearer, who comprise Greenleaf Press, have revised, edited, and updated *Famous Men of Greece*. This work was originally written by John H. Haaren, LL.D. and A.B. Poland, Ph.D. in 1904. Quoting from Greenleaf's preface to *Famous Men of Greece*:

> *When we read about Moses leading a rebellious and grumbling people across a desert, we identify with Moses -- until it is not only Moses that we see, but ourselves, acting under seemingly impossible circumstances. The study of history becomes not merely the study of nations, but a moral training ground where the wise and the unwise are observed, and the consequences of wisdom and folly may be dissected under a teacher who charges less than Experience.*
>
> *Just as the child identifies with Moses, he can also identify with other historical figures and analyze the wisdom and folly of their actions. When at the center of all this is the question, "What does God think about this action, person, behavior?", then the study of history (even the study of very pagan nations) takes place in a way in which the God of History is ever present.*
>
> *We are firmly convinced that biography should be an integral part of a child's study of history.*

Greenleaf Press offers an Ancient Greece study package which includes: *Famous Men of Greece* (mentioned above), *The Greenleaf Guide to Famous Men of Greece, The Greeks* (by Usborne), and *The Children's Homer*. Greenleaf also offers several other titles which can be purchased separately. (For those pinching their pennies, I have found many of the titles they recommend at my public library. After reviewing some of these books at your library, you may decide to purchase them.) I recommend at least buying *The Famous Men of Greece* and *The Greenleaf Guide to the Famous Men of Greece*, which may be purchased separately. (I introduced the *Famous Men of Greece* above.) *The Greenleaf Guide to Famous Men of Greece* walks you through your study while integrating vocabulary, discussion questions, projects, and suggestions for supplementary reading assignments. This guide is well written and I find it satisfies at least two purposes. First, it acquaints us with an important and interesting part of history. Secondly, it offers an excellent example for preparing future historically based unit studies. After familiarizing themselves with Greenleaf's plan of action, parents can follow their model and create units of their own. This idea of copying can enable us to excel in a variety of areas. (As mentioned previously, Greenleaf's catalog is an excellent resource in itself!)

The third book included in the Ancient Greece Study package is *The Greeks*, from the Usborne Illustrated World History Series. This book offers a glimpse at many aspects of early Greece. It will supply you with a variety of additional topical studies to include in your lessons. Areas of interest include: A Greek House, Clothes and Jewelry, Pottery, Architecture, Sculpture, Music and Poetry, The Theatre, Medicine, Greek Myths, and many more. Like all Usborne books, this book is loaded with kid-appeal.

The fourth and final book included in the Ancient Greece study package is *The Children's Homer: The Adventures of Odysseus and the Tale of Troy*, by Padraic Colum. Padraic Colum combines the age old stories from Homer's *Iliad* and *Odyssey* into one enthralling adventure. Published in 1918, Padraic Colum's vivid re-telling of the Greek epics is an excellent introduction to the classic myths for young people.

Greenleaf offers a variety of other interesting books to enliven your study of Ancient Greece. Some titles are available at your public library. Ancient Greece book list: *Cultural Atlas of Ancient Greece*. Includes maps and other useful information pertaining to daily life in Ancient Greece. Recommended for use with junior high aged student. *Journey Through History: Greek and Roman Times*, by Verges. 2nd-3rd grade reading level with a higher interest level. *D'Aulaire's Book of Greek Mythology*. Appealing watercolor drawings depicting the Greek myths. The D'Aulaire's are Caldecott Medal winners. *Bulfinch's Mythology Coloring Book*, available from Greenleaf. *Tales of the Greek Heros*, by Low. This book is beautifully illustrated and a delight to read. (I found this book in the reference section of my public library. Some libraries may own a circulating copy.) *Mythology*, by Edith Hamilton. A good text for junior and senior high school aged students. *The Golden Fleece*, by Padraic Colum. The author of *The Children's Homer*, reviewed earlier, retells the story of Jason's quest for the Golden Fleece. Awarded the Newberry Honor in 1922. *The Trojan*

War, by Coolidge. *The Trojan Horse ... or How the Greeks Won the War*, a Random House "Step-up-to-Reading" book. *Adventures of Ulysses*, by Evslin. *The Iliad*, by Homer. (Penguin edition.) *The Odyssey*, by Homer. (Translated by Richmond Lattimore.) *The Last Days of Socrates*, by Plato. *Ancient Astronomy*, by Asimov. Great for use with young children. *Astronomy Activity Book*, order from Greenleaf. *Ancient Greece*, published by Doubleday.

You do not need to utilize a multitude of books to complete your study. Some books may be used only for their illustrations, others as read-aloud books with your children, some for children to read independently, and some for children to read aloud. Choose one or two books to act as your basic text, such as *Famous Men of Greece* and *The Children's Homer*. The Greenleaf Guide will provide a sufficient number of suggestions to enhance your study. Use other books as they suit your needs, realizing that this study of Ancient Greece can be either a brief introduction or an all absorbing quest.

Greenleaf Press also offers the *Famous Men of Greece Pronunciation Tape*. The names of the people and places found in *Famous Men of Greece* will not become a mess of jumbled syllables with the aid of this tape!

FINE ARTS

ANIMATION UNIT

Most children enjoy drawing, and usually cartoon characters are the first objects they attempt to recreate. This unit is an entertaining unit and a good one to interject between units more academic in nature.

Library Books

Walt Disney, Master of Make-believe, by Elizabeth Montgomery. *Walt Disney*, by Greta Walker. *Walt Disney's Mickey Mouse, His Life and Times. Bill Peet, An Autobiography. Draw 50 Famous Cartoons*, by Lee J. Ames. *Ed Emberley Drawing Books*, some titles are: *Ed Emberley's Great Thumbprint Drawing Book; Ed Emberley's Big Orange Drawing Book; Ed Emberley's Picture Pie, a Circle Drawing Book*. You will find many how-to-draw cartoon books at the library. Investigate the children's section as well as the fine arts section of your public library. Since animation involves the use of a movie camera, you may want to investigate this device. David Macaulay's *The Way Things Work*, includes a brief but concise explanation, with terrific kid-pleasing drawings of the movie camera.

Books

The Big Book of Cartooning in Christian Perspective, by Vic Lockman.

In this unit I have chosen to focus on Walt Disney and Bill Peet. Walt Disney loved to draw cartoon characters and was fascinated with animation, which made characters look as if they were moving. He was making animated cartoon commercials for movie theaters as a young man, but was frustrated because he felt the figures moved too stiffly. He read all the books he could find on animation, and developed a technique which made the characters move naturally. This required making a series of drawings and photographing them. It took much longer, but the animated characters were more lifelike. As you read biographies of Disney, you will learn of the advancements being made while he was perfecting his films. First, sound appeared in movies and then color was introduced. These two topics provide spring boards for further study for those who want to pursue them. You will be amazed at the number of academy awards Disney won for his animated films, true life adventures, and full length motion pictures.

Reading the autobiography of Bill Peet will be fascinating for both you and your children. I stayed up past midnight reading it myself. The book is filled with interesting tidbits. Mr. Peet casually takes us on a stroll through American life during the First World War. He acquaints us with his newspaper selling days as he shouts exciting headlines such as "Lindberg Flies the Atlantic! Extra! Extra! Read all about it!". He gives us a glimpse of the desperate days of the Great Depression, he relates his memories of the great flood of the Ohio River, he recounts Amelia Earhart's disappearance over the Pacific, he reminds us of the Hindenburg disaster, and he tells us of the continuing national problem of unemployment. Later he joins the artists at the Disney studios. He recounts his struggle to rise in the company. Peet gives us a glimpse of what it takes to put together animated films. We learn about drawing in-betweens, composing story boards, developing screenplays, recording characters' voices, and more. In a brief, entertaining way, we experience the animation industry. In the midst of his work at the Disney studios, World War II breaks out and Disney begins producing animated training films, films to sell war bonds, and films to ridicule and vilify the enemy. After the war, work resumed as usual. Peet goes on to write and illustrate children's books. He has written more than thirty picture books.

In his autobiography, Peet explains that he drew pictures in a writing tablet during school. Often he was caught doing this so he began to draw directly in his school books, on the margins of the pages, which was graphic evidence that he spent little time reading the text. At used book sales, Peet's illustrated books were best sellers. He said he supposed those books were the very first ones he ever illustrated for children.

Bill Peet was amazed when Walt Disney asked him to write a feature-length screenplay. He said it was a wonder that he could write much more than his own name after daydreaming and drawing his way through classes in school. Peet attributed his ability in language to his love for books and the hours he spent reading many of the best authors at the neighborhood library.

You will find this a delightfully fun unit to explore with your children. The children could have fun drawing still cartoons and inserting captions with dialogue. Look up animation in an encyclopedia or library book and investigate the techniques of animation. Make an animation booklet, having the children draw a character on each page of a book with the binding at the top. Use the same character on each page, changing the body position very slightly on each page. Then flip very quickly through the book, and the figure will look as if it is moving. Compare this with the information you find on animation in the encyclopedia or library book.

THE ORCHESTRA AND GREAT COMPOSERS UNIT

Music is a delightful avenue to explore with our children. It stimulates creativity and an appreciation for quality entertainment. Often this seems a difficult area to study, because as parents we sometimes lack a good musical background ourselves. This is all the more reason to investigate music with our children. The age of audio electronics has made it possible for us to obtain quality recordings of the great composers at affordable prices.

I suggest making the study two-fold. A brief study of the orchestra along with a study of two famous composers' lives. If you try to study several composers at once, the study can become confusing. Later in the year, or in years to follow, other composers' lives can be studied. You may want to review the instruments of the orchestra or study a particular section of the orchestra in greater depth. I have listed five biographies of famous composers. Select two and enjoy.

Library Books

The Boy Who Loved Music, by David Lasker. Based on an actual incident from the life of Joseph Haydn. This book contains charming illustrations by the author's father, Joe Lasker. *The Twenty Children of Johann Sebastian Bach*, by David Arkin. Contains beautiful illustrations and provides a good introduction to the life and times of Bach. *Ludwig Beethoven and the Chiming Tower Bells*, by Opal Wheeler. Opal Wheeler has written many music biographies and is an interpreter of music to children. Her warm literary style and delicate skill make for pleasurable reading for all ages. This biography was first published in 1942. It certainly surpasses the short, choppy, slick-looking, unfeeling biographies often written for children today. *Handel at the Court of Kings*, by Opal Wheeler. Handel was known as the Father of the Oratorio and was the composer of the magnificent *Messiah*. *Mozart, the Wonder Boy*, by Opal Wheeler. Mozart was a child prodigy. Opal Wheeler has caught Mozart's life-long fascination with children. Thirty-five full pages of Mozart's music are included. *The Pantheon Story of Music for Young People*, by Joseph Wechsberg. Contains an historical overview of western music. Every major composer has been emphasized with a special treatment of the classical and romantic periods. The text is filled with interesting illustrations offering a glimpse at music history. *Great Composers*, by Piero Ventura is similar in content to the book listed above, but is a much more recent publication. This is evident in the illustrations which have a modern look rather than one which captures the feeling of the age as reflected in *The Pantheon Story of Music*. *The Magic Flute*, based on the opera by W.A. Mozart, retold by Stephen Spender. Brief biographical information about Mozart is included at the end of the book. *The Magic Flute* was Mozart's last opera. *Meet the Orchestra*, by William W. Suggs. A lively introduction to the orchestra. The author explores the ancestry of each instrument, then turns to the development of the orchestra as a group and the role of the conductor. *This is An Orchestra*, by Elisa Posell is similar to the book listed above, but treatment is given to each section of the orchestra. Photographs depict the instruments and individuals who play them. Included is a list of suggestions for a Beginner's Listening Library. *Making Music*, by Arthur Paxton. Contains mostly photos accompanied by a simple text relating the idea that music is composed by a person. *Make Music Mine!*, by Tom Walther. A Brown Paper School Book. This book will tell you how to make a variety of appealing musical instruments with your children. It also explains why some sounds are music and others are just noise. (This is intuitive with most mothers!) *The Magic of Music*, by Lisa Weil. An easy introduction to music for young children.

Books and Other Materials

Sower series Biographies: *George Fredrick Handel. Peter Ustinov Read the Orchestra*, by Peter Ustinov, with the Toronto Philharmonic Orchestra. A full-length cassette providing a demonstration of the wide variety of instruments in the orchestra. *Moss Classical Music Tapes*. Tapes include a narration of the composer's life accompanied by selections from his music. Some selections are: *Bach, His Story; Bach is Best; Beethoven, His Story; Beethoven Blockbusters; Brahms, His Story; Chopin, His Story*. Other composers include: Handel, Haydn, Mendelssohn, Mozart, Schubert, Tchaikovsky, and Wagner. Also available are the *Music Masters Series*. There are three sets inclusive of seven composers each. A narrator discusses the composer's life. Representative music of the composer is included. The Cornerstone Curriculum Project offers a full, four year music curriculum consisting of biographical narrative and representative music of the great composers entitled *Music and Moments With the Masters*. (See resource section.) Two games our family enjoys are published by Aristoplay. The first is *Music Maestro II*, a game of musical instruments, past and present. This includes two cassette tapes presenting instrument sounds. The second game is *The Game of Great Composers*, an introduction to compositional style: Medieval to Modern. Contents include a cassette tape of keyboard selections illustrating compositional styles and a composers booklet. Another interesting and less expensive game, is the *Composer's Card Game*. *The Way Things Work*, by David Macaulay offers several sections beneficial to this musical study: Sound and Music, Sound Waves, Amplifier, Electric Guitar, and Musical Instruments. He uses clever drawings and simple text to familiarize us with woodwind, brass, string and percussion instruments. (Watch out. If Dad gets a hold of this book the kids may never see it again!) Another well written book is *The Gift of Music - Great Composers and Their Influence*, by Jane Stuart Smith and Betty Carlson. This book is written from a Christian perspective and contains an enlightening preface by Francis Shaeffer.

I don't suggest purchasing every or even most of the items listed above. If your budget allows I think some of these will add an exciting dimension to your study. The library is a valuable source for recordings of selections by various composers. The value of purchasing your own cassettes is their availability. The narratives of the composers' lives are also helpful.

This study has far more educational benefits than first meets the eye. Geography and history take on a new perspective when viewed through the eyes of the great composers. It is evident that many publishers are turning once again to the study of music and composers, as many products are now available for educational use.

If you or your children play a musical instrument, this unit is a natural. Use these talents to enrich your unit. Several of the biographies by Opal Wheeler contain music by the representative composer. Perhaps your family can attend a classical concert in your area. Video tapes and television broadcasts offer another avenue for viewing and listening to concerts.

Writing assignments naturally flow from this study as the children are inspired to write while listening to the works of the great artists. Interesting passages from the composers' biographies can be copied or taken from dictation. Selections by favorite composers set the mood for children to create visual works of art. Use your imagination and make this unit enjoyable. Remember, it's best to keep things simple and concentrate on one or two composers at a time. You may also choose to study only one section of the orchestra for each unit. Later, when you choose to study one or two more composers, you can investigate another section of the orchestra. The key to a successful unit is simplicity. Simplicity affords the children better retention, the adults less stress, and therefore everyone greater enjoyment!

The impressionists were different from the painters before them. They often left their studios and painted out of doors. They were concerned with capturing the passing moment to create an "impression" of what they saw. The impressionists put the colors on in little dashes and dots. They concentrated a great deal on light and how it made objects look different at different times of the day. They simply tried to spontaneously depict the world around them.

Several years ago I was taking an art class at a nearby college. Our assignment had been to do a detailed charcoal pencil drawing of a landscape. I did a large picture of a park with lots of trees. After looking at my picture, the teacher gave me a fat piece of wet charcoal and a cup of water for dipping. He asked me to use this to recreate in ten minutes what it had taken me four hours to accomplish. Upon completion of my picture he was very pleased and said I had captured the feeling of the landscape much better the second time. He put that picture in the school art show. It was a type of impressionistic expression. Impressionism conveys feelings.

Impressionism may not be your favorite style of art, but it is certainly interesting and worth taking a look at.

Library Books

Pierre-Auguste Renoir, by Ernest Raboff. Raboff, an artist himself, is well known for guiding children through the world of art and artists. He has written many other books. *Young People's Story of Fine Arts, The Last Two Hundred Years*, by V.M. Hillyer. I believe this is now out of print, but many libraries still own copies. There are a number of other titles in the "Young People's Story" series. If you come across any at a used book sale be sure to buy them. *Famous Paintings, An Introduction to Art for Young Readers*, by Alice Elizabeth Chase. An excellent choice for a beginning student for art appreciation. *Great Painters*, by Perio Ventura. A very thorough yet uncomplicated treatment of fine art. Ventura uses his own artistic talents, particularly cartoon-like pictures, to tell the story of the great masters. He includes narrative about the masters and their masterpieces. These books can be used for other fine arts studies as well.

The Impressionist Revolution, by Howard Greenfeld, focuses on Monet, Sisley, and Pissaro. This is a text for the more serious art appreciation student. *Mary Cassatt*, by Nancy Mowll Mathews. Contains beautiful photographs of the works of Cassatt. *Renior*, by Bruno F. Schneider. This book contains beautiful color photographs of Renoir's works. *Degas*, by Edward Huttinger. The works of Degas are depicted in appealing color photographs. *Monet at Giverny*, published by Mathews Miller Dunbar. Includes photographs of Monet's paintings as well as photographs of his family, home, and elaborate garden. *The Impressionists*, by Michael Wilson. Contains reproductions of the works of many of the impressionists. The text is lengthy, however. *Children in the World's Art*, by Marion Downer. Written in a clear simple style, this book focuses on the works of Degas, Cassatt, Renoir, and other artists who used children as their subjects.

Books and Other Materials

Artisoplay has done it again. *Art Deck, the Game of Modern Masters: Impressionism to Surrealism*. 52 different paintings are featured on deck-sized cards. Cornerstone Curriculum Project offers a fine art curriculum entitled, *Adventures in Art*. Many catalog companies offer the Ernest Raboff series of artist biographies. The Classic Plan offers a curriculum integrating fine art, poetry and music. Fine art prints can be ordered directly from the Washington, National Gallery of Art. (See address in resource section.)

For this unit I have chosen to focus on four of the impressionists. Units become too complicated if we try to concentrate on too much at once. Even though we are concentrating on Renoir, Degas, Monet, and Cassatt, we come in contact with many others as we study these people's lives and view the works of many of the impressionists in the library books.

The French Impressionists formed a fellowship and jointly exhibited their works. After some time, they recruited an American woman to exhibit with them. Her name was Mary Cassatt, a great admirer of Degas. Later she was instrumental in gaining American support for Impressionist painting. Mary excelled at painting domestic subjects, mothers with their children, and young girls. This is why I find her work fascinating and an excellent choice for study.

It is often interesting to select a reproduction of a painting by Cassatt from a library book and create a story to accompany it. I find her paintings of mothers and their children particularly well suited for this purpose.

Edgar Degas, unlike his Impressionist contemporaries, showed a partiality to unnatural colors. He used gray and brown to convey dingy urban life and pinks and purples created by theater lighting. Other Impressionists used only colors that appear in nature. Degas' painting centered on all aspects of Parisian life: circuses, racetracks, dance halls, the theater, and of course the ballet. His paintings of the ballet are most appealing. Boys would probably be more interested in his horse race paintings and drawings.

Pierre-Auguste Renoir predominately painted human subjects. He incorporated children, beautiful women, and festive groups into his paintings. He is well remembered for his lovely painting of a "Child with Watering Can." Another favorite of mine is "Girl with a Hoop." As you view the works of the various artists, allow your children to select a favorite painting and share with the family why he or she likes it. Have the child read the history of the chosen work, and present this information to the family as if he were a guide at an art gallery. Look for as many details as possible when observing the paintings. What can you conclude about the people in the picture? Are they happy, sad, confused, angry, or exuberant? Using a thesaurus, try to find a variety of words that describe the painting, focusing on the people, objects, background, and overall tone of the painting.

Every time we mention Monet, my children make some comment about his lily pond. He frequently used his garden at Giverny for his paintings. Monet is noted for having painted haystacks. This may seem an odd subject for painting, but Monet was seeking to capture the effects of light at different times of the day. He painted fifteen pictures of the same haystack. He painted twenty pictures of the front of a French cathedral at various times of day and each picture was different. Monet was not necessarily interested in the shape or form of an object, but in the light and color that could transform an object. Compare Monet's paintings with the other Impressionists. Did they all paint like Monet? Have your children make a list of some of the similarities and differences they note in paintings by each artist. Encourage them to note variations and likenesses in subject matter, mood, color, light, seasons, time of day, location, and so forth. Once again, you don't have to be an art expert to be observant and have an opinion.

In any art study you pursue, you will encounter the human form. The human figure has been a subject of continuous study throughout time. Many of the great masters have tried to capture the grace and perfection of the human body, and often of the nude form. For this reason please use discretion when allowing your children to freely look through books with art reproductions.

Additional Activities

Using library books such as *Young People's Story of Fine Art; Famous*

Paintings, an Introduction to Art for Young Readers; Great Painters; or books in the *Ernest Raboff Series*, read information about the artists and works being studied. Have your children dictate or copy pertinent information about each artist. Using some of the ideas listed above, incorporate writing skills through observations of selected works of the artists you are investigating. Locate the artist's native country on a map. As you read, you should discover some general information about the political climate in which they lived. How did this affect their work? Using some of the more technical library books offering high quality reproductions of the artists' works, observe other paintings by the artists. These books, generally located in the fine arts section of the public library, often have a better and larger selection of artists' works. Occasionally read brief passages from these texts, but do not allow yourself to get bogged down with too much technical information. Remember, keep the unit simple, stress free, interesting, and therefore truly educational. Buy some inexpensive paints (**not** cheap paints) and allow your children to experiment, seeing if they can capture the impressionistic style on canvas. They may choose to paint from real life, preferably outdoors or in a bright, naturally-lighted room, or they may want to copy one of their favorite paintings. The great masters have been copied time and time again by many an aspiring art student. It is this same concept of copying well written literature that provides us with an excellent model. Mom and Dad must also try the paint and brush. You are never too old to learn and have fun.

I suggest buying paints in tubes, whether acrylics, oils, or water colors. The jars and bottles of paint have a short shelf life, and are very messy. Boxed sets of water colors quickly turn to "mud." Just a dab of each color on a piece of aluminum foil will suffice for each child. Purchase a variety of brushes. It pays to invest in middle-of-the-line brushes. Canvases are not cheap, so canvas paper in a pad will do nicely at first. If you have very young children, begin with water based acrylic paints. They are easy to clean up and less expensive than oils or water colors. (Water colors in tubes that is.) Acrylics can be used with a greater amount of water than usual to produce a water-color effect. Any art quality paper may be used with acrylics. Water color paints do better with water color paper, and oil paint work best with canvas paper, canvas board, or stretch canvas.

Make fine art a regular part of your yearly studies. Like music, art serves to stimulate our creativity and helps us appreciate the creative beings that we are, fashioned in the image of the Supreme Creator.

THE PAINTERS OF THE AMERICAN REVOLUTION UNIT

History

This unit focuses on four great painters who lived during the Revolutionary Era. These individuals made artistic contributions which aided in the historic documentation of this era. The four painters are: Benjamin West, John Singleton Copley, Charles Wilson Peale, and Gilbert Stuart. Many other artists' works and lives are reviewed as well, but on a lesser scale.

Library Books

Benjamin West and His Cat Grimalkin, by Marguerite Henry. This is an excellent book. We all enjoyed it so much! *Copley*, by Elizabeth Ripley. *The Pantheon Story of American Art for Young People*, by Ariane Ruskin Batterberry and Michael Batterberry. *American Adventures*, by Elizabeth Coatsworth. In particular, we read the section entitled, *Boston Bells*, a story about Copley. *Painter of Patriots, Charles Wilson Peale*, by Catherine Owens Peare. *The Art of Colonial America*, by Shirley Glubok. *The Art of the New American Nation*, by Shirley Glubok. Look in the fine arts section of your library for books with reproductions of paintings by the four artists mentioned above. Several of the books I've suggested have works included by these artists. To help fill in background material for this unit, we also read a number of other books about individuals who lived in America during the Revolutionary Era. Most of these books were read at bedtime or breakfast. *Carry on, Mr. Bowditch*, by Jean Lee Latham. *Boat Builder*, by Clara Judson. (About Robert Fulton.) *Patrick Henry, Firebrand of the Revolution*, by N. Campion.

Language Arts

This unit requires a lot of reading aloud with your children, and the biographies are entertaining. Since these biographies are filled with dialogue, they are very good for dictation or copying exercises. This gives your children practice with using quotation marks and beginning a new line when a new character speaks. Use this opportunity to allow capable children to read aloud from the biographies. Younger children may narrate a portion of what has been read. This is a great activity for them as it builds vocabulary, expression, and retention of the material being read. Once you have finished reading a biography, the front inside jacket flap makes an excellent selection for your children to copy or take from dictation. This capsulizes the book. Ask your children to write a summary that they would include in the front of the book if they were publishing it. Maybe they feel that some other information should have been added or that some information should have been deleted.

Allow your children to look at the reproductions of the artwork in the library books. Read about the history surrounding the individual paintings. Ask your children to examine a painting done by one of the artists you are studying. Give them two minutes to examine the painting. Then have them make a list of all the things they remember from the painting. This list may include, people, things, places, colors, feelings expressed, and so on. After doing this activity a few times, you can have your children make columns on their papers with headings for nouns, adjectives, and adverbs. Then they can write words describing the painting in the proper columns. Encourage your children to be more descriptive with each assignment. Later, see if your children can relate the story behind the paintings.

Art

Read an account of an historic event from the Revolutionary time period. Have your children illustrate this event with colored pencils, crayons, oil paints, watercolors, markers, or pastels. Then have them give their paintings a title.

GENERAL KNOWLEDGE

Videos

Sign Language for Everyone, by Cathy Rice, includes a 170 page hard-back book.

Public libraries often have sign language videos available. Check with a deaf service center in your area. They usually offer basic signing courses to the public for a nominal fee.

Books

The Joy of Signing, by Lottie Riekehof. Available at Christian book stores. *Sign Language for Everyone*, by Cathy Rice. (The book may be purchased separately from the video tape.) *Hue and Cry*, by Elizabeth Yates, edited by Gloria Repp and published by Bob Jones University Press. A fictional story that takes place in New Hampshire in the 1830's. Jared Austin, a faithful member of the mutual protection society that defends his community against thieves, struggles to temper justice with mercy when his deaf daughter, Melody, befriends an Irish immigrant youth who has stolen a horse.

Library Books

I Have a Sister -- My Sister is Deaf, by Jeanne W. Peterson. This book is illustrated with soft charcoal drawings and provides information on how the deaf compensate. Truly a heart warming text offering a perceptive portrait of a young deaf child. *Anna's Silent World*, by Bernard Wolf. Six-year-old Anna was born deaf. She receives special training in lip-reading and the use of hearing aids. Also available in Spanish, *Ana Y Su Mondo de Silencio*. *Perigee Visual Dictionary of Signing: An A to Z Guide to Over 1,200 Signs of American Sign Language*, by Rod Butterworth. *A Story of Nim: The Chimp Who Learned Language*, by Anna Michel. This book has large print, easy text, and photographs. *Exploring Mime*, by Mark Stolzenberg. *Mandy*, by Barbara D. Booth. A sensitive story about a young deaf girl who doesn't like to go out at night because she can't read lips or signs in the dark. *The Way Things Work*, by David Macaulay. Among many other topics, this book contains interesting and informative material about sound and the ear. *Presenting Reader's Theater: Plays and Poems to Read Aloud*, by Caroline Feller Bauer. A collection of over 50 read-aloud scripts. A short but informative section is included on mime on pages 14 and 15. Select a few plays and have the children mime appropriate parts.

Introduction

Quoting from Timberdoodle's catalog:

Just between us...Did you know that the population of the hearing impaired in the United States alone, is nearly equal to the entire population of Canada? If you find that fact as staggering as we did, then you'll readily see that there may be no more practical second language for your family to master. Plus, American Sign Language fulfills a foreign language requirement in many states!

Terminology

American Sign Language, Manually Coded English, Fingerspelling, Manual Alphabet, Pidgin Sign English, Sign Language, Deaf Persons, Hard of Hearing Persons, Gestuno, etc.

Bible

Using a concordance and/or a topical Bible, locate passages dealing with hearing versus understanding. Example:

"You will keep on hearing, but will not understand; And you will keep on seeing, but will not perceive; For the heart of this people has become dull, and with their ears they scarcely hear, and they have closed their eyes lest they should see with their eyes, and hear with their ears, and understand with their heart, and turn again, and I should heal them." Matthew 13:14,15 (NASV)

Look up other terms in your concordance or topical Bible such as ear, sound, hearers, deafness, etc. Parables are excellent selections for you and your children to pantomime. Remember, no talking allowed. The children have fun guessing which parable is being acted out. Look up pantomime in the dictionary before you begin. You may need to read and review a number of parables before undertaking this endeavor.

Vocabulary

You will begin to build a signing vocabulary, and continue to increase your signing vocabulary in units to follow. This will give added dimension to all your units and will build and maintain skills in signing. It is easiest to stick with signs for simple words at first, like the names of animals.

Storytelling

Relate short stories using sign language. This is different from pantomime because the story is told using actions and sign language, not actions alone. Signed storytelling videos are often available at colleges, video rental stores, and public libraries. Watch one and see if you can interpret the story.

Arts

Mimes, Clowns

Costumes

History of mime

Slow motion and robot movements

Skit writing

Science

Ear

Larynx

Sound

Hands (Hands play an important role for the deaf person. Signing is also very good for increasing hand coordination and mobility.)

Choose some simple library books that explain about the ear and how it works. David Macaulay's book, *The Way Things Work*, is an excellent choice. Your library probably owns a copy, but it may be located in the adult section. This is a book well worth purchasing as it can be used with almost any unit that relates to science. The pictures are great for those of us who need to see something to understand it. The text is brief yet thorough.

History

The history of signing can be learned by reading biographies.

Gallaudet, Friend of the Deaf by Etta DeGering and *A Deaf Child Listened* by Anne E. Neimark are both excellent biographies of Thomas Hopkins Gallaudet

"Cobblestone: Helen Keller/America's Disabled" May 1983, *A Picture Book of Helen Keller* by David A. Adler and *The Story of My Life* by Helen Keller all contain interesting information about the life of Helen Keller. (The library will have detailed as well as very simple biographies of Helen Keller.)

90

Middle Ages: Monks during this era used signing when they took a vow of silence. Early Bibles have been found with signs drawn in them.

Music

Today we find more interest in signed interpretation of music. This portrays lyrics, rhythm, and emotions of songs. This form of expression helps deaf people and hearing people to enjoy and experience music together.

Language Arts

Give your children a spelling test and have them fingerspell the words. Write skits to be performed by pantomime. Dictate or copy selections from the books you have chosen. Write a letter using pictures of signs to convey your message. Fingerspell words for your children and have them write these words as you spell them. Write a description of a fair, carnival, or some other usually noisy affair from the perspective of a deaf child. Write a letter to the organizations listed below for information about deafness.

Activities

Visit a nursing home and communicate with the deaf patients. They are happy even if you only fingerspell with them. Have your children sign a song or a Bible verse for them. Choose their best pantomime of a parable and have the children act it out.

Let signing be the only communication between you and your children for a specified length of time. Try 30 minutes. It's interesting to see how they try to get your attention and how frustrated they become when they can't easily do it. Discuss how discouraging it might be at times for deaf children to live in a world of silence.

Have children draw the handpositions to spell their name. A good reference book for this activity is *The Handmade Alphabet* by Laura Rankin.

Sources for Information

Gallaudet University
800 Florida Avenue, N.E.
Washington, DC 20002

Registry of Interpreters for the Deaf, Inc.
51 Monroe Street, #1107
Rockville, MD 20850

KIDS CREATE A UNIT

I decided it was time for each of my children to plan a unit that appealed to their individual tastes. We spent a week discussing choices while finishing up another unit. They changed their minds several times during the week of discussion. I explained why some units would be more difficult than others, and that some topics needed to be narrowed down as they were too general. Once they had made up their minds, we visited the public library. I helped each child search for appropriate books. Yes, this did take time. We spent over three hours. You must realize, however, that I was helping four children hunt for books, and our busy two year old was also "helping."

THE CIVIL WAR

Michelle, my oldest daughter, chose to study the Civil War time period. Her fascination with the clothing of that time enticed her to make that era her topic of study. One of the books relating to clothing that she chose was *Corsets and Crinolines*, by Norah Waugh. Another was *Uniforms of the Civil War*, by Francis A. Lord and Arthur Wise. For her project, she made a dress from that era. Other books selected were: *The Art of America from Jackson to Lincoln*, by Shirley Glubok. *I Varina, A Biography of the Girl Who Married Jefferson Davis and Became the First Lady of the South*, by Ruth Painter Randall. *Abraham Lincoln*, by Ingri and Edgar Parin d'Aulaire. *Ulysses S. Grant, Encyclopedia of Presidents*, by Zachary Kent. *America's Robert E. Lee*, by Henry Steele Commager, illustrated by Lynd Ward. I read *Invincible Louisa*, by Cornelia Meigs to my older girls. This is the Newberry Award Winning biography of Louisa May Alcott, the author of *Little Women, Little Men* and many other titles. She lived during this era and served as a nurse in a Union hospital for a short time. Her relationships with wounded soldiers spurred her to write articles for a newspaper concerning their lives. Miss Alcott was acquainted with Ralph Waldo Emerson, Henry Thoreau, and Henry Wadsworth Longfellow. Reading the writings of some of these men added a literary flair to the study.

My daughter selected several fiction books based on true accounts from the Civil War. *Phantom of the Blockade*, by Stephen Meader. *Across Five Aprils*, by Irene Hunt. *North by Night*, by Peter Burchard. *Uncle Tom's Cabin*, by Harriet Beecher Stowe. *Rifles for Watie*, by Harold Keith. (Newberry Award

Book.) *Freedom Crossing*, by Margaret Goff Clark. Two fictional books relative to this time period were purchased from a Christian book distributor. They were *The Dixie Widow* and *The Last Confederate*, both by Gilbert Morris. (These are books eight and nine in the Winslow series.)

As we began to investigate this era, we realized we could study for several months, even years! The main emphasis was to become acquainted with this time period, and in the future more in depth studies would prevail.

One important thing to realize when undertaking a study like this is that when you read the biography of one individual, many individuals are brought to light as they interact with the biographee. It is not necessary to read dozens of biographies for each unit you pursue.

My daughter also checked out a video on the Civil War. Each day Michelle read from a selected book and wrote a paper concerning her findings. Some days this was a summary of what had been read, and other days this was a selection she chose to copy from one of the books. Each evening she would share some interesting bit of information with the family. For her project, she chose to make a dress from the time period. Initially she wrote to an historical pattern company seeking information. After receiving the pattern, she selected fabric and began to make the dress. She even made wire hoops! (The historical pattern was ordered from Amazon Dry Goods. See resource guide.)

For another project Michelle wrote a simple, fictional play situated in the South during the Civil War. This play was based on the book, *Freedom Crossing*. She made full color plates depicting the costumes of each character. She designed the clothes using costume books from the library and an Amazon Dry Goods catalog.

I feel that this study is a good example of how a specific unit can be tailored to fit a student's interests. Most of the library books were located by using the subject card catalog. Others were found by using a reference book entitled *American Historical Fiction and Biographies for Children and Young People*, by Jeanette Hotchkiss.

DOLLS AND STUFFED TOYS

My next daughter, Melissa, chose to undertake a unit on dolls and stuffed toys. She selected some books on making dolls, doll houses, and stuffed toys. She also chose some storybooks relating to those topics. She decided to study

A.A. Milne's *Winnie-the-Pooh* books in particular. The following are titles of the books Melissa chose: *William's Doll*, by Charlotte Zolotow. *Dollhouse Mouse*, by Natalie Standiford. *Bear and Mrs. Duck* by Elizabeth Winthrop. *Katherine's Doll*, by Elizabeth Winthrop. *The Best-Loved Doll*, by Rebecca Caudill. *Satchelmouse and the Doll's House*, by Antonia Barber. *Winnie-the-Pooh, The House at Pooh Corner, The World of Pooh, and The Pooh Storybook*, by A.A. Milne. She also read a biography of A.A. Milne. *Edith and the Bears, A Gift From the Lonely Doll, and The Lonely Doll*, by Dare Wright. *Making Your Own Toys*, by Pamela Peake, *Dolls and Toys from A to Z*, by McCalls Needleworks and Crafts. *Creative Soft Toy Making*, by Pamela Peake. *Dollhouse Magic*, by P.K. Roche. *Dollhouse People*, by Tracy Pearson. *The Pooh Craft Book*, by Carol Friedrichsen. *Hittie, Her First Hundred Years*, by Rachel Fields. She also located a number of story books about dolls by Rumer Godden. She enjoyed these the most.

Melissa chose to make a stuffed doll. She selected a pattern from a library book and used graphing techniques to enlarge the pattern. She calculated the amount of material needed and purchased it. After she made the doll, she wrote and illustrated a book featuring the doll as the main character. She also wrote each day from the books she read and shared information from her studies with the family. Melissa typed the front jacket flap information from each library book. She is maintaining a folder with this information from each book she reads.

CONSTRUCTION

My younger boys, Robert and Raymond, decided to conduct a unit together. They chose construction. Since my boys are only 8 and 6 years old, we didn't study this topic in great detail. We selected some simple books for Robert to read to Raymond and me. Other books were chosen primarily for their illustrations.

Library Books

Round Buildings, Square Buildings, & Buildings That Wiggle Like a Fish, by Philip M. Isaacson. *Stone and Steel*, by Guy Billout. *Tunnels, Up Goes the Skyscraper!*, and *Tool Book*, all by Gail Gibbons. *Towers and Bridges*, including simple experiments, by Julie Fitzpatrick. *Pyramid, Castle, Cathedral*, and *City*, all by David Macaulay. Our library has the video *Castle*, based on

Macaulay's book. *The Ultimate Wood Block Book*, by Sam Bingham. *What It Feels Like to Be a Building*, by Forest Wilson.

We purchased an impressive book called *The Art of Construction, Projects and Principles for Beginning Engineers and Architects*, by Mario Savadori. Even I was able to understand the principles described in this book. It includes projects that use ice cream sticks, paper, string, paper clips, and so forth to demonstrate construction principles. My husband and I read selections from this book to the boys.

Robert read the simpler books, like those by Gail Gibbons, to Raymond and me. Then I asked the boys questions concerning these books. I chose sentences for them to copy. They circled the phonics rules in each word and we discussed these rules along with pertinent punctuation and capitalization rules.

The boys looked for examples of the construction principles we studied in things around us. For example, they looked for triangles in objects. Triangular formations give a structure support. They found some of these formations under the seats of chairs, on the bottom of stools, in bicycle frames, in the swing set, and in roof trusses.

My boys really enjoy playing with Lego blocks, which fit right in with their studies. We also used the library book, *The Ultimate Wood Block Book*, and my husband helped the boys make the special blocks described in the book. (We eventually bought a copy of this book because it was so fascinating.) These blocks were used to make a variety of projects in the book, including castles, bridges, and other engineering marvels. The interesting structures are not only appealing to children, but they also incorporate accurate construction principles.

Robert and Raymond each dictated a story to me that was in some way related to building. Robert's story was entitled, *The Tiny Builders*, and Raymond's story was called, *How to Build a Castle*. Each day I would neatly write out several sentences from their stories and the boys would copy them, read those portions aloud to me, and circle the phonics rules in each word. It was through this process that my younger son, Raymond, began to show a great improvement in his reading ability. He was certainly pleased with himself.

Take some time out to allow your children to create their own units. The experience will be both educational and rewarding.

ABOUT THE AUTHOR

Valerie is the wife of Bruce Bendt and the mother of their five children, Michelle, Melissa, Robert, Raymond, and Mandy. This is Valerie's second book and companion to her first, *How to Create Your Own Unit Study*.

Her most recent publication, *Creating Books with Children*, is a manual designed to help parents make memorable books with their children.

Valerie is available to speak on the following topics: How to Create Your Own Unit Study, How to Get the Most from Your Public Library, Teaching Math K-3rd Grade with the Hundred Board and Creating Books with Children.

For information concerning workshops, or for questions or comments pertaining to unit studies write to:

Valerie Bendt
333 Rio Vista Court
Tampa, FL 33604

RESOURCE GUIDE

RESOURCES

The materials I have referred to in this book are listed here with appropriate addresses. I suggest that you write to each company for a catalog.

AMAZON DRYGOODS
2218 E. 11th Street
Davenport, IA 52803
(800) 798-7979

Over 1,000 historic, ethnic, and hard-to-find clothing patterns.

AMPERSAND PRESS
691 26th Street
Oakland, CA 94612
Games: AC-DC, O'Euclid, Kril, The Pollination Game, and more.

ARISTOPLAY
P.O. Box 7529
Ann Arbor, MI 48107

Games: **Where in the World?, Music Maestro II, The Game of Great Composers, Art Deck, Somebody, Hail to the Chief, Made for Trade, Constellation Station, Land Ho!/Tierra Tierra!, Pyramids and Mummies, By Jove and By Jove Stories**, and other titles.

AUDIO MEMORY PUBLISHING
1433 E. 9th Street
Long Beach, CA 90813

Audio cassettes: Geography Songs, More Geography Songs, & many others.

BACKYARD SCIENTIST
Jane Hoffman
P.O. Box 16966
Irvine, CA 92713

Backyard Science Series I, II, and III.

BOB JONES UNIVERSITY PRESS
Greenville, SC 29614

Hue and Cry, by Elizabeth Yates. The story of a deaf girl living in New Hampshire in the 1830's. Bob Jones also carries many other fine publications and a complete line of text books.

CLASSIC PLAN

20969 Ventura Boulevard, Suite 213
Woodland Hills, CA 91364

A fine arts curriculum integrating music, poetry, and art.

COMMON SENSE PRESS

P.O. Box 1365
8786 Highway 21
Melrose, FL 32666
(352) 475-5757

Learning Language Arts through Literature series, elementary through high school. *The Common Sense Reading Program,* first grade skills. *The Great Editing Adventure Series, The Reading Skills Discovery Series, Bookshelf Collections, Math Sense Building Blocks Program, 100 Sheep, Grocery Cart Math, 3-Way Math Cards,* and *The Wordsmith Series. Creating Books with Children, For the Love of Reading, Frances Study Guide, How to Create Your Own Unit Study, Success With Unit Studies,* and *The Unit Study Idea Book,* by Valerie Bendt. *We Home School,* by Debbie Strayer. *How to Teach Any Child to Spell/ Tricks of the Trade,* and *How to Home School.*

Note: New Homeschooling resources are available. Contact your Common Sense Press Dealer for new product information.

CORNERSTONE CURRICULUM PROJECT

2006 Flat Creek
Richardson, TX 75080
(214) 235-5149

Music and Moments with the Masters, Adventures in Art, Making Math Meaningful, Science the Search, and more.

CROSSWAY BOOKS

Division of Good News Publishers
Westchester, IL 60153

Books Children Love: A Guide to the Best Children's Literature, by Elizabeth Wilson. *Teaching Children: A Curriculum Guide to What Children Need to Know at Each Level Through Sixth Grade,* by Diane Lopez. *For the Children's Sake,* by Susan Schaeffer Macaulay. *The Gift of Music,* by Jane Smith and Betty Carlson.

DOVER PUBLICATIONS, INC.

31 East 2nd Street
Mineloa, NY 11501

EVAN-MOOR CORPORATION
18 Lower Ragsdale Drive
Monterey, CA 93940

How to Make Books with Children. Grades 1-6.

GOD'S WORLD PUBLICATIONS
P.O. Box 2330
Ashville, NC 28802

God's World Newspapers, kindergarten through adult levels.

GREENLEAF PRESS
1570 Old La Guardo Road
Lebanon, TN 37087
(615) 449-1617

Great resources for historically based units. *The Greenleaf Guide to Ancient Egypt, Famous Men of Greece, The Greenleaf Guide to Famous Men of Rome, Famous Men of the Middle Ages,* and *The Greenleaf Guide to Famous Men of the Middle Ages.*

HOMESCHOOLING TODAY
P.O. Box 1425
Melrose, FL 32666
(904) 475-3088

A bi-monthly magazine designed specifically for homeschooling families and those who take an active role in their children's education. Practical, easy-to-understand, and ready-to-use ideas are presented for every age group. In addition, each issue features a full color pull-out art lesson, which alone is worth the subscription price. *Homeschooling Today* magazine offers the tools and encouragement needed to facilitate homeschooling and to enhance family life.

HOUGHTON MIFFLIN COMPANY
215 Park Avenue South
New York, NY 10003

David Macaulay's books: *Castle, Cathedral, City, Pyramid, Underground, Unbuilding,* and *The Way Things Work.*

INSTITUTE IN BASIC LIFE PRINCIPLES
Box One
Oak Brook, IL 60522-3001

Character Sketches: Volume I, II, and III.

"From the pages of Scripture, illustrated in the world of nature."

INSTITUTE FOR CREATION RESEARCH
P.O. Box 2667
El Cajon, CA 92021

Scientific Creationism, by Henry Morris. ICR publishes many fine texts pertaining to the wonders of creation.

THE KNOWLEDGE OF THE HOLY

By A.W. Tozer. "A classic Christian testimony and devotion."
Available at Christian book stores.

MOTT MEDIA
1000 East Huron
Milford, MI 48042

The Sower Series consist of biographies of historical figures written from a Christian perspective. Some titles include: *Abraham Lincoln, Robert E. Lee, George Fredrick Handel, Samuel F.B. Morse, Isaac Newton, The Wright Brothers, Noah Webster*, and more.

NATIONAL GALLERY OF ART
Washington, D.C. 20565

Send for fine art print catalog.

NATIONAL GEOGRAPHIC SOCIETY
Dept 1675
Washington, D.C. 20036

Exploring Your World, the Adventure of Geography; National Geographic Picture Atlas of Our United States.

"SIGN LANGUAGE FOR EVERYONE"
4 Hour Video Tape
Bill Rice Ranch Films
Murfreesboro, TN 37129
(615) 893-2767

THE TEACHING HOME
P.O. Box 20219
Portland, OR 97220-0219

A Christian magazine for home educators. Specific issue concerning **"Using the Library,"** April/May 1990.

USBORNE BOOKS
EDC Publishing
10302 East 55th Place
Tulsa, OK 74146

Usborne publishes a multitude of colorful books with loads of kid-appeal. Some titles include: *Early Civilization, Pharaohs, and Pyramids, World History Dates, Explorers, Knights and Castles, Introduction to Physics, Introduction to Biology, Fashion Design, Lettering and Typography, Photography, Weather and Climate, Understanding Music, The Usborne Story of Music, The Usborne Story of Painting, Drawing, The Young Astronomer, Bird Life, Ocean Life, Space Facts, Plant Life*, and many more.

ACKNOWLEDGEMENTS

Portions taken from the preface to *Famous Men of Greece* and *The Greenleaf Guide to Ancient Egypt*, page 4, are used with permission by Greenleaf Press, Lebanon, Tennessee.

Portions taken from *The Institutes for Biblical Law*, page 262, are used with permission by Ross House Books, P.O. Box 67, Vallecito, California, 95251.

Portions taken from *Scientific Creationism*, page 18 are used with permission by the Institute for Creation Research.

Portions taken from *Exploring Your World, The Adventures of Geography*, page 148 are used with permission by the National Geographic Society.